D0021638

The

MISSING
MIDDLE

THE
MISSING
MIDDLE

*Working
Families
and the
Future of
American
Social
Policy*

THEDA SKOCPOL

*A Century
Foundation
Book*

W. W. NORTON & COMPANY
New York • London

The Century Foundation, formerly the Twentieth Century Fund, sponsors and supervises timely analyses of economic policy, foreign affairs, and domestic political issues. Not-for-profit and nonpartisan, it was founded in 1919 and endowed by Edward A. Filene.

Copyright © 2000 by the Century Foundation
All rights reserved
Printed in the United States of America
First Edition

For information about permission to reproduce selections from this book, write to Permissions, W. W. Norton & Company, Inc., 500 Fifth Avenue, New York, NY 10110.

The text of this book is composed in Berling with the display set in Peignot Demi.
Composition by Chelsea Dippel
Manufacturing by The Maple-Vail Book Manufacturing Group
Book design by Charlotte Staub

Library of Congress Cataloging-in-Publication Data

Skocpol, Theda.
       The missing middle : working families and the future of American social policy / Theda Skocpol.
              p.   cm.
       "A Century Foundation book."
       Includes index.
       ISBN 0-393-04822-5
       1. United States—Social policy—1993–   2. United States—Politics and government—1993–   3. Working class families—Government policy—United States.   4. Middle class families—Government policy—United States.   I. Title.
HN65.S5635   2000
361.6'1'0973—dc21   99-37842
                                                                              CIP

W. W. Norton & Company, Inc., 500 Fifth Avenue, New York, NY 10110
www.wwnorton.com

W. W. Norton & Company Ltd., 10 Coptic Street, London WC1A 1PU
1 2 3 4 5 6 7 8 9 0

CONTENTS

FOREWORD

SOME MAY THINK that this is an odd time to focus on the issue of inequality: the popular press describes the present as the best of times for many Americans. Overall, this is a period of remarkable prosperity, but what is striking is that even after the long-sustained economic upswing of the 1990s, the United States still has the greatest inequality of wealth and income in the developed world. One of the reasons for this situation is obvious: Most of the increase in wealth in the past decade involves the appreciation of financial assets—and such assets are the most unequally distributed part of personal wealth.

Yet few in American politics want to rain on the current parade. The battle, rather, is over who can take credit for low unemployment rates, steady growth, and a federal budget surplus. These are, to be sure, important and memorable accomplishments, but it does not diminish them to focus on the persistence of poverty and inequality, the lack of health care for millions of Americans, unequal access to educational opportunity, and other problems that undermine our overall sense of social welfare. The successes that we are enjoying could and should be the impetus for attacking the problems that continue to afflict so many.

We owe much to Theda Skocpol for our understanding of these issues. In a body of work over the past two decades, including *Boomerang: Health Care Reform and the Turn Against Government, The New Majority* (coedited with Stan Greenberg), *Civic Engagement in American Democracy* (coedited with Morris Fiorina), and *Protecting Soldiers and Mothers: The Political Origins of Social Policy in the United States*, she has documented and explained how such diverse events as the creation of pensions for Civil War veterans in the nineteenth century and the passage of Social Security in the twentieth spring from common characteristics in our national politics and personality.

In this volume, Ms. Skocpol brings together her exceptional knowledge of the history of social policy and her keen sensitivity to political realities at a critical time for social programs in the United States. Following the enactment of the most sweeping changes in welfare programs since the Great Depression, the central topics of American politics have become the need to reform Social Security and Medicare. It is not an exaggeration to say that the outcome of the struggle over these programs will reshape the agenda of both parties for a generation. *The Missing Middle: Working Families and the Future of American Social Policy* provides a lucid explanation of these issues and of the other key elements of contemporary progressive policy. It explains the nature of America's necessary struggle to redress inequality and reduce its consequences and offers a blueprint for those who seek a renewal of long-standing traditions of broad-based social programs for all Americans. Ms. Skocpol's ideas are compelling. And they are practical, representing the sort of thinking of real value to policy makers and political leaders.

The Century Foundation believes that this subject is so important to our nation's future that we have devoted much of our energy over the past several years to bringing it to the public's attention. We have supported such works as James K. Galbraith's *Created Unequal: The Crisis in American Pay*, Edward N. Wolff's *Top Heavy: The Increasing Inequality of Wealth in America*, Joel F. Handler and Yeheskel Hasenfeld's *We the Poor People: Work, Poverty, and Welfare*, and *No One Left Behind*, the report of a

Century Foundation Task Force on retraining America's workforce. In a belief that there is a need to ensure that this critical subject remains in the public eye, we are currently supporting works by Barry Bluestone (and the late Bennett Harrison) on how inequality and flawed public policy undermine economic growth; a study of skill, work, and inequality by Edward Wolff; an examination of the impact of technology on economic inequality by Simon Head; and an examination of what the United States can learn from other countries about the workforce, economic inequality, and public policy by Jonas Pontusson.

The unpleasant truth is that one does not have to be a cynic to say that if something is being ignored in the public sphere, that means there is no political gain to stressing it. In other words, in the market for political discourse, where there's a potential "profit," there will be active market participants. Maybe. But unlike the easy calculations of wins and losses in commerce, politicians often have a tin ear when it comes to what the public wants to hear or what the nation really needs. Theda Skocpol believes, in effect, that such a misunderstanding is at work, and she makes a powerful case that a renewed progressive agenda—one that stresses the obligations that we have to include those least fortunate in social programs that benefit a broad spectrum of the population—is not only morally compelling but also politically feasible. This message is of great import. On behalf of the Century Foundation, I thank her for this timely work.

RICHARD C. LEONE, President
The Century Foundation
April 1999

PREFACE

FOR YEARS I HAVE WORKED with students and associates to understand the politics of U.S. social provision—from the emergence of public schools, veterans' pensions, and programs for mothers and children in the nineteenth and early twentieth centuries, through the fashioning of social insurance and antipoverty programs in the New Deal and the Great Society, to the rise and demise of Bill Clinton's Health Security effort in the early 1990s. Drawing from what I have learned about the possibilities and shortfalls of the past, this book grapples with current U.S. policy debates, asking how we as Americans can continue to care for our grandparents while doing a much better job than we now do of supporting all working parents as they do the hard and vital work of raising our nation's children.

Again and again, throughout our national history, we Americans have created and sustained generous, dignified, and democratically grounded social programs to support families and offer enlarged opportunities to individuals. But in recent decades, our national politics has veered off course, turning away from the kinds of social programs and political strategies that previously worked so well for so many. A "missing middle" has emerged in American social policy and political debates, as we argue about supposed trade-offs between helping young and old, while failing to address the values and needs of working parents who are at the vortex of contemporary societal changes. Advocacy groups debate artificially polarized positions, while politicians resort to symbolic gestures rather than measures that could really help regular families of modest means.

Can the citizens of the United States find ways to revitalize our best traditions of democratic social provision? The obstacles are many, and I face them head-on in this book. In the end I argue that, yes, we Americans can revitalize our best traditions of inclusive social provision to meet today's challenges and forge a bright shared future.

This book has taken a while to come together, as I have wrestled with the hopes and frustrations of social policy debates and progressive politics in the 1990s. For patience as well as advice, I am grateful to people at both W. W. Norton and The Century Foundation. I would also like to thank the many colleagues who worked with Stanley Greenberg and me on the "New Majority project" of 1995 to 1998. Whether they know it or not, they served as unpaid consultants, giving me many good ideas about how progressive politics might be revitalized. For excellent research assistance and advice during the final stages of this project, I am grateful to Jillian Dickert (who is not responsible for the things I continue to say here with which she disagrees!). And, as always, I have been very fortunate in the support and inspiration of my husband Bill Skocpol and my son Michael Skocpol. Through several summers in Maine, they put up with my preoccupation with this project.

THEDA SKOCPOL
Mount Desert, Maine

The
MISSING
MIDDLE

CHAPTER ONE

The Missing Middle

"**WE'LL PUT GOVERNMENT BACK** on the side of the hard-working middle-class families of America who think most of the help goes to those at the top of the ladder, some goes to the bottom, and no one speaks for them."[1] With this bold promise, Governor Bill Clinton of Arkansas announced his run for the presidency in October of 1991. "Putting People First" became the watchword as Clinton and vice-presidential candidate Al Gore were nominated by the Democratic Party and waged their ultimately successful 1992 campaign. Bemoaning twelve years of Republican-dominated government rewarding "those who speculate in paper," while "the forgotten middle class worked harder for less money" and "the working poor had the door of opportunity slammed in their face," Clinton and Gore advocated a change of direction toward a federal government newly active on behalf of regular Americans—and especially working parents. "Putting our people first means honoring and rewarding those who work hard and play by the rules. It means recognizing that government doesn't raise children—people do."[2]

Economic growth with social equity and health care coverage for all Americans would be the top priorities, Clinton and Gore proclaimed. Welfare reform would be accompanied by job training and measures to ensure higher wages and enhanced social protections for all working families. Along with new incentives

3

for market investments would come substantial public "investments" in community infrastructure, improved schools, and expanded access to higher education. Shrinking the federal deficit would be a goal, but not at the expense of social improvements. Economic growth would be channeled by new regulations designed to reduce income disparities, discourage "outrageous executive pay," and make the rich "pay their fair share in taxes."[3] Clinton and Gore also promised to break with old ways of doing politics. "Our political system failed us," they declared, vowing to transform a system "dominated by powerful interests" and "high-priced influence peddlers."[4]

Nearly a decade later, Americans can look back on not just one but two Clinton presidencies that have been politically very successful—arguably even triumphant in the face of the Congressional "Republican revolution" of 1994–95 and the impeachment proceedings of late 1998 and early 1999. At the height of his Senate impeachment trial, President Clinton delivered his next to last State of the Union address. He took credit for eliminating the federal budget deficit, putting the nation "on course for budget surpluses for the next 25 years," and achieving "the longest peacetime economic expansion in our history—with nearly 18 million new jobs, wages rising at nearly twice the rate of inflation, the highest home ownership in history, the smallest welfare rolls in 30 years—and the lowest peacetime unemployment since 1957."[5] Clinton outlined a plan to devote projected federal surpluses to retiring federal debt and shoring up Social Security and Medicare in order to "meet our generation's historic responsibility to establish true security for 21st Century seniors." He added a long list of proposed regulatory and tax adjustments, most justified as ways to help "our children" prepare for the "21st Century economy."

Conspicuously missing from the 1999 State of the Union address were the "forgotten middle class" and the "working poor" so prominently featured in 1991 and 1992. Listeners might imagine that there are no longer Americans lacking basic social pro-

4

tections or working "harder for less money." But actually economic and social inequities have continued to widen during the 1990s, just as they did during the previous twelve years presided over by Republican presidents Ronald Reagan and George Bush.

To be sure, all Americans have benefited from steady and robust economic growth. In the expanding economy of the 1990s, men and women have been able to find jobs—even combine two or three jobs to buoy family incomes. Real increments to the wages of low- and middle-income employees finally appeared late in the 1990s expansion. But by far the greatest part of the decade's economic gains have flowed toward the most privileged heights of the American class structure—not to put too fine a point on it, toward those who "speculate in paper" on Wall Street.[6] The incomes and wealth of the top fifth have soared, with the top 5 percent (indeed the top 1 percent) doing best of all. As economist Lester Thurow explains, "the bottom 60 percent of Americans cannot benefit from the stock market boom since they don't own any stock." And wages have also stagnated for nonprivileged Americans. "Real wages for 80 percent of the male labor force are below where they used to be," Thurow notes, adding that incomes for families right at the middle of the U.S. income ladder have hardly changed in real dollars since the 1970s, even though "the average wife is working 15 more weeks a year than she did back then."[7]

At the bottom of the economic ladder the American dream of success through hard work is fading, explains political scientist John Schwarz, because "more than 12 million full-time year-round workers are paid wages beneath those needed to support a minimally decent standard of living for households with children. Two-thirds of workers who start at subpar wages are unable to lift themselves to a decent wage even after a decade of full-time work."[8] Nor can families working for meager pay count on adequate health care, pensions, or family leaves. Huge gaps remain in social supports vital to the well-being of working families. Private employers have reduced contributions to employee retirement pensions and health insurance for employees and their family members. Less-educated Americans working for low or modest wages are the least likely to be covered, and are the ones experiencing the sharpest cutbacks in employers' contributions to health insurance and pensions.[9] Many of these same working men and women remain beyond the reach of federal legislation.

Under the 1993 Family and Medical Leave Act that President Clinton repeatedly touts as one of his and the Democratic Party's major legislative achievements, employees of small businesses (who are more likely than other employees to earn low wages) are not covered at all. And the legally covered employees of larger enterprises must be able to afford to forgo wages if they want to claim their right to take unpaid time off to tend to family emergencies.[10] For many of America's most vulnerable workers, political advertisements touting Family and Medical Leave as a great step forward must simply underline the irrelevance of government to their daily lives.

People working for low or modest wages and their children are also the ones falling through the cracks in our nation's ever-more-fractured and incomplete health care system. Leaving aside the many employees who must contribute more to employer-designated managed care plans that may not meet their needs, the ranks of Americans not covered at all by any private or public health insurance rose from 14.8 percent of the nonelderly population in 1987 to 18.3 percent in 1997.[11] Despite President Clinton's support for the principle of extended coverage, about one million Americans per year have lost health insurance during his watch; and contractions in public coverage account for much of the increase in the uninsured since 1993. By 1997, more than 43 million Americans had no health insurance—and coverage shrinks the lower down the income ladder one goes. Although Medicaid subsidizes care for many of the needy, nearly one-third of all impoverished Americans were uninsured in 1997. Most Americans not covered by health insurance are members of families with at least one worker; and the uninsured include about half of impoverished full-time workers.[12] These working Americans play by the rules, yet go without a basic social support vital to personal and family well-being.

Of course, we cannot simply blame the Clinton administration for shortfalls of social policy during the 1990s. After Clinton took office in 1992, progressives inside and outside of government had to contend with federal budget deficits and fierce conservative and business opposition to new social initiatives. When President Clinton's "Health Security" initiative failed, Republican "revolutionaries" led by Newt Gingrich took control of Congress and proceeded to slash spending for many social programs.[13] But here is the point: Over the last few years, the federal budgetary situation has eased and conservative firebrands have been tamed, yet President Clinton shows little sign of taking up the unfinished business of "putting people first." By any measure of popular well-being, the "health care crisis" is worse than in 1992. But who in or near the Clinton-Gore administration now speaks about the mounting numbers of Americans lacking basic health insurance coverage—or going without other employment benefits or social supports necessary to family security? Who in power ever even mentions the widening gaps in income and opportunity that have accompanied the 1990s economic boom? President Clinton—and his heir apparent, Al Gore—have stopped talking about the "forgotten middle class." And they are no longer tackling the toughest issues of social equity.

The basic trouble lies in the shape of American public discourse and the lay of the land in U.S. politics. For all that he is an adroit defender of established federal programs, Bill Clinton has led Democrats and the nation toward accommodating rather than challenging today's dominant political realities: big money influence; a shrinking, class-tilted electorate; and public debates dominated by professionally run advocacy groups. The social issues Clinton has featured since the mid-1990s resonate closely with agendas of public discussion set by clashing advocacy groups and media pundits—who themselves reflect and take for granted a constricted and increasingly class-biased political universe.

American social policy debates these days are notable for concentrating on the elderly versus the young. Advocates are especially likely to argue over the merits of public programs for the retired elderly *versus* efforts to aid very poor children—saying little about the needs of the vast numbers of working parents who are truly at the epicenter of the changing realities of U.S. society and economic life. Conservatives in and around the Republican Party champion tax cuts favoring privileged families and entrepreneurial individuals. "New Democrat" politicians—urged on by the Democratic Leadership Council—espouse regulatory adjustments and tax credits that, in practice, help privileged employees more than others. Meanwhile, self-declared liberals limit themselves to defending special programs for the poor or pushing for a bit more public help to underprivileged children—who are often discussed apart from their working parents. Too often lost from view in these debates are Americans of the missing middle.

I mean "middle" in both a socioeconomic and a generational sense. The people of the missing middle are working men and women of modest economic means—people who are not children and not yet retirees. They are the adults who do most of the providing and caring for the children who represent the future of American society, while paying the taxes that sustain retirees now and into the future. What is more, as Bill Clinton correctly suggested back in 1991 and 1992, Americans in the missing middle are not exclusively "the poor" on whom many liberals and conservatives debating welfare chiefly focus. Still less are they the biggest market winners, the entrepreneurs and investors and wealthiest professional families whose achievements and needs are championed by conservative Republicans—and by many "new Democrats," too. These Americans are, above all, the people who put in long hours to earn a living and make a decent life—coping with rising pressures in their workplaces, while trying to raise children in solo-parent or dual-worker households.

PUNDITS AND PEOPLE AT ODDS

Not only are the needs of such Americans in the middle often ignored, these citizens also hold commonsense values at odds with the polarized positions dramatized by advocates and politicians who capture the attention of the national mass media in an era of restricted politics. Questions of family integrity and security worry many people, yet the instincts of everyday Americans are at odds with the pronouncements dominating our national airways and editorial pages. The most visible pundits, advocates, and politicos are often not on the same wavelength as regular citizens—particularly not when the issue is the role of government and community in supporting families amidst economic and demographic upheaval.

Most Americans, for example, believe that our nation can and should preserve Social Security and enhance Medicare as dignified and shared protections for the elderly. The majority want such steps to be taken for existing social insurance programs at the same time as our nation undertakes improved efforts to ensure educational opportunity, job security, and health care for all working-aged adults and their children. Although wary of government waste and unnecessarily high taxes on ordinary families, Americans consistently tell pollsters that they don't want cuts in social supports used to pay for tax cuts for the wealthy. Indeed, many Americans have said they would be willing to pay a bit more in taxes, if they could be sure that new resources would not be wasted and would be devoted to basic goals like preserving Social Security and ensuring health care for all.[14] People want a variety of family supports to be cautiously pursued, with government very much involved along with local communities, businesses, and religious congregations.

Despite such popular attitudes, many advocates and politicians

pursue restrictions on government as the overriding goal for contemporary public policy. Lip service may be paid to the goal of a
balanced federal budget, but many politicians make sustaining a
long-term balance ever more difficult by pushing tax cuts or credits favoring the wealthy and the professional-managerial upper
middle class. Tax reductions must happen, we are told, because
Americans in general are inherently hostile to doing things
through government. Yet a sober reading of democratic opinion
suggests that most Americans of modest means very much want
certain things done through government.

To further agendas of tax-cutting or the breakup of public programs, right-wing advocates and politicians encourage popular
disillusionment with government and overstate the degree of
existing distrust among citizens of modest means. Americans
today certainly do wonder whether elected politicians are taking
their priorities and values into account. This may be especially
true for parents, 57 percent of whom recently agreed with the
statement "I don't think public officials care much about what
people like me think."[15] But if people could have things as they
wish, many would like a federal government that focuses on dignified social supports for families: sustaining Social Security and
Medicare, ensuring safe communities, enhancing educational and
job opportunities, and ensuring basic health care and access to
child care and other supports for all working families.[16] Americans would like new public initiatives to address the struggles of
working mothers and fathers, especially those with modest
means.[17]

Not just conservative Republicans but advocacy groups billing
themselves as "nonpartisan" tout drastic cuts in social spending as
the only way to the promised land of a "balanced" federal budget and a growing economy. For example, backed by generous
funding from Wall Street and echoed by its many admirers in
the elite media, the Concord Coalition—an advocacy group of
budget-balancers and self-appointed fiscal watchdogs led by
investment banker Peter Peterson—insists that the future of "our

children and grandchildren" depends on slashing "entitlements" for middle-class retirees. Prognosticating crisis from an inevitable "demographic tidal wave," the Concord Coalition urges drastic changes in Social Security and Medicare, and predicts doom for the young if we don't slash federal "entitlement" spending.[18] Editorialists have joined the Concord Coalition and many other advocacy groups in calling for elected representatives to be "courageous" by voting for cutbacks in social programs for the elderly, changes that voters have clearly said they do not want. Some liberals go along with such reasoning, hoping that public resources can be reallocated from the elderly to better fund endangered programs for the poor and the young. Opponents of social insurance routinely urge Americans into the trenches of a generational war that most people do not want to fight—a struggle that average Americans correctly sense to be entirely unnecessary.

The debate over "family values" is another area where elite and popular opinion are frequently in noncreative tension. Most Americans worry about both the material circumstances *and* the moral climate for family life today. After all, real incomes for most working Americans, especially the young adults responsible for children, have declined or merely inched upward since the early 1970s.[19] Opportunities to get steadily ahead at work are hard to find for many without college educations. During recent decades, an ever-more-commercialized and libertarian culture has undercut marital commitment and made sheltering and guiding children more difficult.[20] Crime and physical insecurity plague many families both materially and morally. Worries about deteriorating schools combine with concerns about access to higher education, which is at once ever-more-costly and ever-more-necessary if young people are to flourish. In short, ordinary families face unprecedented material *and* moral challenges—and most Americans know it.

But, strangely, many opinion-making elites are arguing about whether today's problems for families are about economics *or* values. Leftists and labor union leaders insist that "America needs a raise," and at times seem to imply that this obviously necessary step would be enough, that higher wages along with more job-connected benefits would solve all family problems.[21] Even less convincingly, some commentators of a culturally conservative persuasion suggest that everything is materially hunky-dory for the vast majority of Americans, that the "real crisis" is about moral values.[22] In this rendition, "values issues" are presented as purely cultural, or as matters of sheer individual willpower and choice (as in "people can choose to play by the rules or not"; "teenagers can choose to have sex or not"; and "women can choose not to have babies when they can't get married or afford to raise them"). In this one-sided view, people suffer materially when they make poor choices—for example, to get divorced or raise a child out of wedlock.

Average citizens perceive the changing family forms of late-twentieth-century America through different lenses than polarizing advocates. To be sure, everyday folks worry about dangers to children born outside of marriage; and many are concerned about youngsters being raised by divorced parents (frequently mothers making do on their own with paltry resources). Public worries about the consequences of family fragility are genuine, even though many Americans are themselves divorced or unmarried parents, and nearly everyone knows friends or family members who are raising children alone. Yet a certain middle-of-the-road sobriety prevails about these family realities. People affirm the ideal of two married parents as best for children, yet at the same time want our schools, communities, and nation to take realities into account, to do the best we can for all parents and children. Ordinary Americans affirm long-standing family values, yet approach present-day departures from them in a spirit of sympathy, not vindictiveness.

Egged on by a media that magnifies glib extremes, clashing advocates insist on falsely polarizing family issues. Traditionalists want America to make divorces very hard to obtain, assuming that this legalistic step will undo tensions between men and women that prevent or dissolve marriages.[23] Meanwhile, some liberals insist that single motherhood expresses feminine independence, or brings salvation to mothers and children who would otherwise suffer abuse. In some circles, stressing the value of married parenthood—or suggesting that America could do more to support this ideal—can end up being denounced as "antifeminist."

Polarized debate about changing family forms furthers a misleading menu of policy options. Even if many poor children must suffer in the short run, say militant "pro-family" conservatives, the United States must not only abolish welfare but also refuse any other kind of support for single-mother families, lest we "subsidize" the morally improper lifestyles of unmarried parents. Some leftists, meanwhile, celebrate pure freedom of choice for adults. They insist that all public policies must further an individualistic version of women's liberation, paying little attention to the limits and supports any society needs to create good environments for raising children. Others simply reduce social policy to welfare, and call for America to concentrate anew on helping the poorest single-mother families, while ignoring the needs of other parents and children.

In the final analysis, most Americans would like our society to discuss broadly shared social problems, focusing on the needs and aspirations of regular folks who go to work every day and try to help their children get ahead in a fast-changing world. The vast majority of Americans live on their wages and make modest incomes—between the roughly $17,000 for a family of four that marks the "poverty line" and the roughly $50,000 a year for a family of four that marks about 25 percent more than the middle point of American family incomes. Most American mothers now work outside the home (as well as in it), yet many take part-time jobs that allow time for care and supervision of children; and many single mothers would like to have this option, too. Most Americans live in apartments or modest homes, and can afford only limited vacations. Ordinary families have to worry about access to good education for their offspring. Most worry about the realm of home and children *and* about the world of work and careers; people don't see these as alternative things to care about. But one would hardly know about the life circumstances and actual worries of ordinary Americans by listening to domestic political and policy debates over the past couple of decades.

In addition to being falsely polarized in all of the ways I have just surveyed, the terms of debate have been tugged steadily rightward by those seeking to slash government and reward the most privileged with tax cuts. Right-wingers have been only weakly countered by new Democrats, or by liberals who engage in rearguard defense of existing government programs or speak only about "helping children." The middle has been left outside contemporary social policy debates, because neither right nor left has much to say about the real-world situation of the vast bulk of ordinary American families who live by wages and salaries, espouse moderate social values, and struggle with the new stresses that families now must face.

Consider especially what has happened on the so-called conservative side of the national political spectrum. As late as the early 1960s, American conservatives were champions of national community along with a strong military. But over the past several decades, since the Civil Rights revolution of the 1960s, a new breed of right-wingers has launched all-out war against the federal government. Crystallizing their cause during the presidency of Ronald Reagan—and carrying matters to an even more absurd extreme under the mid-1990s crusades led by militant House of Representative leaders Newt Gingrich and Dick Armey—contemporary conservative Republicans have championed the cause of slashing the size and scope of extralocal government. Lip service may be paid to the ideal of a "balanced federal budget," but the real aim of conservative Republicans is to hobble the domestic federal government and cut taxes on the well-to-do. This is done in the name of unleashing the free market and establishing what Newt Gingrich calls an "opportunity society" that rewards—and celebrates—America's most privileged individuals and families.[24]

"Family values" are touted by conservative Republicans, and not just to palliate their popular allies in the Christian right. Sincere and eloquent statements about basic moral concerns are often made by today's conservatives. Yet when it comes right down to it, conservative legislators propose measures disproportionately helpful to Americans clustered in the top third of the class structure. Benefits flow to families whose incomes derive from very high salaries, property holdings, and capital investments. Conservatives want to cut the taxes and subsidize the investments of such already well-off people because they honestly perceive such families as right-living—good models for all Americans. What is more, they believe the efforts of such model citizens will help all of us, by promoting vigorous market growth.

Under the conservative program, however, the tab for dwindling social supports and public sector necessities must be borne by other American families—especially those getting by on modest wage and salary incomes and relying in retirement on Social Security and Medicare. Lower taxes for the rich leave Americans who live by wages and salaries shouldering ever more of the tax burden, even as educational loans, health coverage, and pensions become less reliable. Deterioration of public services and benefits, combined with the tougher tax bite on work rather than capital investments, can in turn be used to stoke popular disillusionment about government. Much commentary about government-slashing and tax-cutting has concentrated on the relative harms imposed on the very poorest Americans. But the real costs fall on the vast bulk of working middle-class families, not just the very poor. And the price is as much civic as material, because citizens who feel their basic values and needs are not addressed soon become cynical about politics and public social provision.

Democrats may realize that cutting taxes on the wealthy—while squeezing Social Security, Medicare, and other federal

15

spending—hurts the very voters on whom their party must depend at election time. But over the past decade or so, Democrats have become less certain of their core values and premises. Popular political participation and voting have dwindled, and Democrats have become increasingly beholden to wealthy campaign contributors. Self-styled "new Democrats" now join Republicans in a litany of complaints against "big government," voting regularly for tax cuts that favor the privileged only a little less obviously than the changes preferred by Republicans. In contrast to many Republicans, new Democrats want to use government regulations and tax credits to channel market forces. But new Democrats frequently demonize "big government" in terms not unlike the excoriations of conservative Republicans. Moreover, rightward-leaning Democrats often end up championing tax reductions and toothless regulations that help, at best, only the top two-fifths of families. New Democrats may favor a broader group of "winners" than contemporary Republicans, yet in practice they deliver little more than rhetoric to most working families.

In and beyond the Democratic Party exists a remnant of unrepentant liberals. Of course, "liberal" is anything but a clear-cut label these days, for it encompasses many who are essentially elite libertarians—people who champion causes like abortion rights or unrestricted civil liberties. Old-fashioned liberals who care about inclusive social programs are a dwindling species, and many of them now rely on a cautious, salami-slice approach to public debate and social legislation.

Since the defeat of universal health reform in 1993–94, socially minded liberals tend to presume that expensive and inclusive new social programs are impossible. Many try, instead, to appeal to public sympathy by arguing that children should be helped as a separate category. Advocacy groups such as the Children's Defense Fund believe that upper-middle-class and corporate support is most likely to be forthcoming for social programs framed as "saving children" or "investing in America's future."[25] From time to time, popular majorities tell pollsters that they want support for both working parents and their children at the same time—for example, health insurance for the working poor, not just for poor children apart from their parents.[26] But this does not change the "realistic" political equation in the minds of many liberal politicians and advocates. At once cheap and publicly appealing, public initiatives aimed at poor children seem like the surest bets at a time when the terms of public debate on fiscal fundamentals and the overall scope of government have been ceded to conservatives.

Liberal wariness may seem understandable, but it can lead to little more than marginal adjustments within a shrinking set of public social supports for American families. In early 1999, for example, the Clinton administration recognized that health insurance coverage for American children has continued to erode despite the Children's Health Insurance Program enacted in 1997. What was the President's response, at a moment when he knew the federal government projected surplus revenues long into the future? He announced the creation of a national toll-free telephone number to provide information about programs for children to parents, many of whom themselves lack or are losing health insurance![27] As this maneuver suggests, solely child-focused liberalism is not a bold position. Hardly a realistic way to address fundamental issues of social equity, this approach speaks much too indirectly to the values and needs of the majority of working American families. Most worrisome, child-focused liberalism does little or nothing to activate millions of American working adults who need support themselves, and who must become civically involved if the political status quo is to change.

ISSUES FOR THIS BOOK

With a focus primarily on national-level public policy, this book seeks to explain how the late-twentieth-century United States has ended up with an artificially polarized, rightward-tilt-ing politics that downplays the needs and values of citizens in the missing middle.

It wasn't always this way. The United States, I will show in Chapter Two, has a long history of generous, inclusive, and popular public social provision. Again and again, this nation has followed a recognizable formula to develop and sustain social supports for large numbers of individuals and families. But in recent times Americans have lost sight of long-standing approaches to successful social policy making.

Sharp disagreements among advocates seeking to reshape U.S. social policies raise fundamental questions to be explored in the core chapters of this book. Many claim that America is doing too much for the old. An array of think tanks and advocacy groups argue that public benefits for elderly people who are not impoverished necessarily hurt the economy and undercut prospects for the young. What are the facts? Are the U.S. elderly mostly well-to-do? Are they receiving unneeded benefits that hurt younger Americans? If changes need to be made in existing social programs for retirees, what reforms would correct previous shortcomings without creating new ones? How could desirable changes become politically feasible? These are issues that I will take up in Chapters Three and Five.

Condemnations of inclusive social protections for America's elderly are profoundly misguided, I maintain. America's social insurance protections for the elderly have had an enormously positive impact on the well-being and civic involvement of our grandparents, including the less privileged. Equally important, Social Security and Medicare have proved morally legitimate and politically sustainable in the U.S. democracy. Social Security should be protected—indeed, extended—for the future, and problems with Medicare addressed in the context of strengthening health care for all Americans.

In very different ways to be sure, both conservatives and liberals tend to justify their schemes for reconstructing U.S. policies by appealing to the needs of "America's children" or the future of "our children and grandchildren." What is actually happening to America's children in the variety of families and communities that make up our diverse nation? I will take up aspects of this huge topic in Chapter Four. What sorts of problems for America's children are caused by broad economic forces and deficiencies of income? Which problems are more attributable to shifts in family lives, including the withdrawal of parental efforts and resources? Are the stresses faced by younger American families today primarily due to high levels of taxation, or market forces, or cultural trends?

In fact, combinations of economic and sociocultural forces are at work. Government efforts to help children and families have not always been effectively focused, and revised efforts, blending certain conservative and progressive ideas, could do much better. As I elaborate in Chapter Five, the United States needs a new vision of opportunity and family security for all, interlocking public and nongovernmental measures focused above all on the needs and values of ordinary working parents.

By one path or another, discussions of what is good for children quickly lead us toward consideration of pressures on American parents. Most American working parents must make a living from wages, salaries, and fringe benefits that are anything but secure in today's fast-changing global and national economy. They must also contend with a commercialized culture celebrating consumption and individual self-realization—values that, if carried to extremes, devalue social commitments and undercut responsible parental efforts to guide children.

Current policy debates shortchange average working parents by arguing obsessively—and unrealistically—about existing government programs versus idealized market solutions. Liberals regularly call for federal governmental activism along the lines of existing antipoverty programs, while most conservatives place supreme faith in unleashed—indeed, additionally subsidized—market forces. With the partial exception of the Christian right, which stresses churches and charities, current policy advocates tend to downplay the importance of social ties of caring and support.

Yet even civically minded conservatives have a stunted view of community, for they treat it as an outgrowth of pure voluntarism. The Christian right and secular civic conservatives speak of voluntarism and charity in sheer opposition to government, suggesting that whenever government withdraws or does nothing, charity and social care will automatically flourish.[28] This is simply false, both historically and now. Historically, as we are about to learn, effective U.S. social policies have often worked through symbiotic ties between government and locally rooted membership associations. What is more, governmental regulations or income supports are often necessary prerequisites of family well-being and flourishing civic ties.

Societal ties—and their absence or breakdown—are affected as much by what happens in the market economy as they are by what happens in the realm of government and politics. Civic conservatives celebrate voluntarism and charity as well as strong families and local communities. But they are suspiciously silent about the many ways in which U.S. market forces and business practices have undermined families and communities. Both government and the market have effects on family and community relationships that need to be analyzed and taken into account as social policies are designed.

POLITICS MATTERS

Throughout this book I analyze the historical and political contexts within which social policies are made or changed. Too often, policy debates take place only in terms of technical schemes or moral absolutes. Professional experts argue over ideal blueprints for programs that might solve technically defined problems—without ever considering whether broad democratic understanding and political support could be garnered on behalf of their idealized policy plans. Advocates argue in terms of moral absolutes—for example, for or against "the welfare state" or "the market"—without taking responsibility for the complex social alliances and political compromises that would be necessary to fashion any successful and sustainable solution to America's social and economic problems. Both technocrats and moralists, moreover, expostulate without any sense of history. Yet good policy making for America's future needs to take into account what has worked, or not, in the past, and how social and political conditions are changing over time. We as citizens need to think with historical insight and political purpose about what might be possible as well as desirable in American democracy—possible if not tomorrow, then within a generation, over the next couple of decades.

The values and policy goals I advocate have been espoused, at least rhetorically, by some Democratic Party politicians—by Bill Clinton in his moments of "putting people first" and by Congressional Democrats who have waged election campaigns around a "Families First" agenda. But the policy ideals and political strategies I offer in this book are, to put it politely, more robust than the often marginal or merely symbolic gestures that most politicians have been willing to put forward. My proposals are certainly much more robust than anything recently elected Democrats have been able to deliver. If Democrats and other progressives really mean what they say about putting families first, they will have to project a more morally compelling vision, develop better policy ideas—and, above all, engage in an extensive strategy of popular political mobilization. Only in this way, as I will sum up in Chapter Five, can American politics and social policy making be recentered on the needs and values of the missing middle.

This book, in short, deals not only with societal trends and public policies. It also reflects on the conflicts, shortcomings, and possibilities of American domestic politics at the dawn of a new century.

CHAPTER TWO

*How Americans
Forgot the
Formula for
Successful
Social Policy*

DEBATES ABOUT THE FUTURE of American social policy
are oddly polarized. Advocacy groups argue about the young versus the old. Liberals focus on the desperate plight of the very
poor, while conservatives celebrate the achievements of the privileged. And all the while the needs of working families of modest means fade from view. Why are national debates patterned
this way? Some would say that inescapable imperatives are at
work—especially the pressure of an aging population and constraints on federal expenditures. But thinking about America in
comparison to other advanced countries suggests that these arguments are misleading.

Across all of the Western democracies, not just in the United
States, citizens are contemplating changes in public social programs, responding to budgetary limits and new social realities. Yet
the changes contemplated in Europe are much more modest than
those advocated by U.S. conservatives, and when Europeans cut
social spending they are trimming welfare states that were more
comprehensive in the first place. Americans complain the loudest
about taxes and limits on public budgets, even though our taxes
are very low by international standards and the United States is
relatively unburdened with public debt.[1] This was true even in
the period right after the Reagan administration of the 1980s

ran up huge federal deficits. By now, the federal deficit has been eliminated—at least on paper—and Democrats and Republicans are arguing over what to do with huge projected surpluses.

Nor is the "graying" of America's population quite the overwhelming problem it is often made out to be. Americans certainly are getting older on the average, but the United States is experiencing comparatively *less* demographic aging than other countries. America stands out compared to European nations— and also in contrast to Canada—for the prominence of arguments that oldsters are "getting too much."[2] But there are relatively fewer elderly people in America than in European countries; and there are projected to be proportionately fewer American elderly in 2025 than there will be elderly Canadians, Europeans, or Japanese.[3] Population aging is a bigger problem elsewhere, but we Americans seem to be the ones most worked up about it, judging from voices prominent in our public debates.

Most puzzling of all is why our policy debates deal so little with the fate of working families of modest means. In recent decades, such U.S. families have suffered much more income decline and erosion of basic social protections than comparable families in Europe and Canada.[4] By "objective" economic criteria, American public debates should be obsessed with what to do about the declining wages of less-skilled workers and the deteriorating security of families earning less than median incomes. This kind of debate has not happened yet—because a nation's politics and public debates are not simple responses to economic realities.

In fact, conflicts about the shape of any nation's social policies are historically and politically rooted. Agendas of public discussion—that is, arguments about problems and possible solutions— arise in relation to things that have previously happened, or failed to happen in that country. The history of social policies is never just dead and gone. What has come before—as well as what might have occurred, but did not—influences political arguments in the present. Proposals for reforms are put forward by groups and leaders engaged in ongoing political battles with one another; and those battles have a history, too.

Before dissecting trends since the 1960s, let us look further back into America's past. A bird's-eye view shows recurrent strengths of nationwide social policies in American democracy. By understanding why major social programs once worked so well, we gain a new perspective on what has gone awry in recent decades. Americans used to know how to create and sustain generous social policies—programs that enhanced opportunity and security for many ordinary families—but in recent decades long-standing successful approaches have not been repeated. What was the historic formula for success in American social policy—and why have we lately lost sight of it?

THE FORMULA FOR SUCCESSFUL SOCIAL POLICY

Conservative polemicists often imply that there have never been any successful social policies in the United States. Americans, assert conservatives, are at heart rugged individualists who don't want any benefits or services from government. This is nonsense. While Americans certainly value individual initiative, and have always disliked "welfare handouts" for very poor people who appear not to be striving to solve their own problems, Americans have again and again shown enthusiasm for generous and honorable social benefits that support people who serve the community and the nation.

Conservatives are not the only ones offering a misreading of America's past. At the other extreme of the spectrum, leftists argue that the United States has never had a true "welfare state," which to them means a comprehensive set of economically redistributive social programs favoring workers and the poor—ideally programs achieved by an organized industrial working class and a labor-oriented political party. True, the United States has never developed a European-style "full-employment welfare state." But this does not mean that popular and generous social policies have been absent in American democracy. On the contrary, such policies have flourished repeatedly—according to a political formula for social policy success that stands in contrast to many features of welfare-state building in Europe.

I am not speaking of "success" in merely technical economic terms. Of course it is important to ask whether public policies are (in the economists' phrase) "cost effective," whether they improve people's lives materially and provide a good value in return for the societal resources invested in them. But cost-benefit calculations can be very narrow; they can overlook matters of moral and political import. In America, as in any democracy, citizens need to have faith in social policies. To be truly workable, social programs must express widely shared values, must find support from broad swatches of the citizenry. And programs must also be well implemented by the particular sort of government a country has. Successful policies by this definition have payoffs for society that go beyond narrowly technical or economic advantages.

While some might quibble a bit, most would agree that the following have been among America's finest social policy achievements. Each of these milestones (whether one program or a set of related measures) has made life much better for many individuals, families, and communities; each has also garnered broad and enduring popular support.

In *public education*, the United States was the first nation in the world to establish popularly accessible common schools. During the nineteenth century primary schools and then secondary schools were founded in most localities and states.[5] During an epoch when only elites had access to education in many other nations, ordinary Americans (except in the South) had routine access to elementary schooling, and many could attend high school and college as well.

Civil War benefits offered disability and old-age pensions, job opportunities, and social services to millions of veterans and survivors of the massive Union armies that fought and won the Civil War. By 1910, more than a quarter of all American elderly men (and more than a third of men sixty-two years and older in the North) were receiving regular payments from the federal government on terms that were extraordinarily generous by the international standards of that era.[6] Many family dependents also got help. Federal spending on pensions took up from a quarter to 40 percent of the national budget in the decades around 1900.

Programs to help mothers and children proliferated during the 1910s and early 1920s. Forty-four states passed laws to protect women workers, and also enacted mothers' pensions to enable poor widows to care for their children at home.[7] In 1912, the U.S. Congress established the Children's Bureau, and at the Bureau's urging Congress passed the 1921 Sheppard-Towner Act to fund health education programs open to all American mothers and babies.[8]

The *Social Security Act* was passed in 1935; subsequently Old Age Insurance (OAI) became the most popular of several provisions in the original legislation. OAI eventually expanded to cover virtually all retired employees, while providing survivors and disability protections as well.[9] Modeled in part on Social Security, *Medicare* was added to the system in 1965 to help pay the hospital and doctors' bills of elderly retirees.[10] By the 1970s, the Social Security system as a whole provided pensions and health coverage for virtually all retired elderly or disabled Americans who were previously regularly employed or were members of the families of such regular employees.

The *GI Bill of 1944* offered a comprehensive set of disability services, employment benefits, educational loans, family allowances, and subsidized loans for homes, businesses, and farms to 16 million veterans returning from World War II.[11] "Little GI Bills" subsequently extended similar, though less generous, benefits to those who served in Korea and Vietnam. GI benefits of one sort or another eventually reached about half of all American families during the 1950s and early 1960s.

Although these giant systems of social support developed in different historical periods and varied in crucial ways, they share four key features. Each has been popularly understood as a reward for service by individuals to the nation, or as a way to help individuals prepare to contribute in the future. Broad cross-class constituencies have grown up around each set of programs; and voluntary associations have worked with government to champion and administer the relevant policies. Finally, reliable and expanding public revenues have been available to fund each set of programs. These four characteristics—which I shall briefly elaborate in turn—add up to a formula for social policy success in American democracy. Until recently, this formula has worked again and again.

Benefits for Service

Successful social programs in the United States have never been understood either as poor relief or as mere personal "entitlements." Socially provided benefits have been morally justified as a return for service to the community, or else as preparation for individuals who would subsequently contribute to the larger community.

The rationale of social support in return for individual service has been a characteristic way for Americans to combine their deep respect for individual freedom and initiative with due regard for the obligations that all members of the national community owe to one another. Citizens who serve the community should not, Americans believe, be dependent on charity or public poor relief. People have to pitch in, but in return it is acceptable for the nation to support and reward them.

A clear-cut rationale of return for service was invoked for the veterans' benefits expanded in the wake of the Civil War and again after World War II. In the words of the 1888 Republican Party platform, social benefits for Union veterans "should be so enlarged and extended as to provide against the possibility that any man who honorably wore the Federal uniform shall be the inmate of an almshouse, or dependent upon private charity. . . . [I]t would be a public scandal to do less for those whose valorous service preserved the government."[12] In a slightly different twist, the GI Bill of 1944 and other benefits for soldiers returning from World War II were justified not only as a response to soldiers' sacrifice but also to ensure the future capacity of surviving veterans to contribute to society. As President Franklin Roosevelt explained, we at home "owe a special and continuing obligation to these men and women in the armed services. . . . Every day that the war continues interrupts the schooling and training of more men and women, and deprives them of the education and skills which they would otherwise acquire for use in later life. Not only the individual welfare of our troops, but the welfare of the Nation itself, requires that we reverse this trend. . . . We must replenish our supply of persons qualified to discharge the heavy responsibilities of the postwar world."[13]

Obviously, benefits for military veterans and their survivors are justified as a return for service to the nation. But this approach doesn't just apply to veterans' benefits. Analogous service rationales have regularly been invoked for other social programs, starting with the nation's public schools. Americans of the late twentieth century tend to think of schools as mechanisms for teaching skills and ensuring a bright economic future for individuals. But the educational reformers and local community activists who originally established the nation's "common schools" argued that children needed to be prepared for democratic citizenship. They held that community schools would give all pupils the disciplined character traits necessary for virtuous civic participation as well as for responsible contributions to workplaces and families.[14]

In the wake of the feminist movements of the 1960s and 1970s, late-twentieth-century Americans often downplay the value of domestic work and unpaid motherhood. But back in the early 1900s, when maternalist programs including Sheppard-

Towner were enacted, they were justified as a support and just return for the services of good mothers. Mothers sacrifice for the community and the nation just like soldiers, reformers argued in the early 1900s. In an era when childbirth could bring death, women risked their very lives to become mothers; and those who lived contributed years of effort by raising healthy and well-socialized children to become the citizens and workers of tomorrow. As Mrs. G. Harris Robertson explained in a 1911 speech to the National Congress of Mothers, we "cannot afford to let a mother, one who has divided her body by creating other lives for the good of the state, one who has contributed to citizenship, be classed as a pauper, a dependent. She must be given value received by her nation, and stand as one honored."[15]

Today's Social Security (and Medicare) system likewise has a profound moral underpinning in the eyes of most Americans. Of course, employees along with their employers channel regular payroll taxes into the Social Security and Medicare trust funds. So retired beneficiaries tend to believe that they have "earned" their pensions or medical care by virtue of contributions over their working lifetimes. But contrary to the claims of many pundits and economists, the exchange everyday Americans perceive is *not* a narrowly instrumental swap of taxes for returns-with-interest on an individual investment account. Rather, Americans understand Social Security and Medicare as just returns from society for the lifetime of work each "contributor" gives to sustain families, communities, and the nation. Each generation is supposed to make such contributions, and then persons enjoy in return a decent retirement and old age. The dignity of work, even humble work for modest wages, is the most important value here.[16] Most Americans see Social Security and Medicare as benefits they have individually earned through work as well as payroll taxes. These benefits are understood as flowing from a social contract enforced by, and for, contributors to the national community.

Broad Constituencies

Successful social programs have built bridges between more and less privileged Americans, bringing people together—as worthy beneficiaries and contributing citizens—across lines of class, race, and region.

Even if major social programs started out small compared to what they eventually became, their contributions and benefits tend to be structured in an inclusive way. Financed by broad-based taxes, successful social programs have delivered support to more and less privileged Americans from the start. Successful social policies have not been structured—or justified—as "welfare" programs, even if sooner or later some of these programs delivered proportionately more help to people who were very economically needy. Broad social programs may have ended up helping the poor, but they covered broad swathes of the citizenry.

Public schools, for example, have been in principle open to all children, not just the offspring of privileged families, as was originally the case with schools in other nations. Civil War benefits and the GI Bill were available to all eligible veterans and survivors of the war in question. Each of these milestone veterans' programs ended up delivering aid to millions of Americans from humble economic backgrounds, including members of racial and ethnic minorities with little political leverage at the time. Among the recipients of Civil War benefits were some 186,000 African American Union soldiers or their survivors, including many former slaves.[17] And the GI Bill of 1944 is credited with opening the doors of even the top American colleges and universities to thousands of young men from humble backgrounds or large families who previously would never have been able to even dream of such opportunities for higher education.[18]

Some early U.S. social programs for mothers and children were restricted to the needy. Mothers' pensions, for example, were supposed to aid widowed mothers who became impoverished after the death of a husband and father who was the family's breadwinner. But around 1900, virtually any American mother who lost a breadwinner husband could suddenly find herself in dire economic need. What is more, other early 1900s programs were universal in their intended scope; they built bridges across lines of class, race, and ethnicity, and between urban and rural areas. The U.S. Children's Bureau was established in 1912 to "investigate and report . . . upon all matters pertaining to the welfare of children and child life among all classes of our people."[19] Similarly, the Sheppard-Towner Act of 1921 was deliberately tailored by Children's Bureau Chief Julia Lathrop to be open to all American mothers, not just the neediest. The "act is not a charity," declared an explanatory clause written during the Congressional debate on Sheppard-Towner.[20] Lathrop reasoned that if the services of Sheppard-Towner were not open to all, they "would degenerate into poor relief." She explained that the new program was "designed to emphasize public responsibility for the protection of life just as already through our public schools we recognize public responsibility in the education of children."[21]

Social Security (including Medicare) is today's best example of a social program with a huge cross-class constituency. True, back in 1935 the contributory retirement insurance provisions of Social Security actually left out many of America's poor, especially African Americans, because domestic workers and agricultural laborers were initially not covered.[22] Social Security originally covered only about a third of U.S. employees, especially those in industrial and some white-collar jobs. By the 1950s, however, Social Security had expanded to incorporate service and agricultural employees. And from the start, more and less privileged employee groups were brought together in this system. It was not just "workingmen's insurance," still less was it a program for the poor alone. Over time, more and more groups of employees were added, both very low wage groups and more privileged sets of white-collar employees, until Social Security became virtually universal for employed Americans.

By the 1970s, Social Security had evolved into this country's most effective program for pulling people out of poverty. This happened, interestingly enough, even though Social Security is not popularly regarded as a "poverty program." Social Security has a broad constituency crossing class lines, and its benefits are understood by Americans as honorable for all citizens to receive.

Partnerships between Government and Civic Membership Associations

Successful social policies have been nurtured by partnerships between government and popularly rooted voluntary associations. There has been no zero-sum trade-off between state and society, and no simple opposition of national government to individual initiatives or local community efforts.

Government has, of course, enacted and administered all of the milestone social programs surveyed here. Even so, a close look reveals how much the development of each policy owes to social movements and voluntary associations that promoted and shaped it in partnership with elected politicians and government officials. Government and voluntary associations together fashioned these policies. Voluntary associations have often pushed for the milestone programs in the first place; in turn the programs have encouraged the growth and involvement of popularly rooted voluntary groups.

These groups include not only nonprofit social service agencies but *membership* associations as well. Although social service agencies have often been involved in helping to administer U.S. social programs, the civic associations that have nurtured major American social programs have usually been membership groups such as women's associations, farm or labor groups, veterans' associations, and church-related associations. In addition to having strong roots in local communities, such membership associations often include regular state, regional, and national activities as well. Indeed, many of these civically active membership associations—such as the Woman's Christian Temperance Union and the American Legion—have been federations that span thousands of localities and parallel the three levels of U.S. government—local, state, and federal. At their base, they have involved individual citizens, groups of neighbors, and very often a range of family members. Fellow citizens have done things with one another in these associations, and at the same time have extended charity to nonmembers and to the needy. These days, it is fashionable to talk about "volunteerism" in American social provision. But, all too often, this turns out to be a euphemism for charitable projects run by nonprofit social services. However, the "voluntary groups" that truly championed and shaped major U.S. social programs in the past were citizens' groups, not primarily agencies for delivering charity or social services.

For example, if we were to go back to the decades prior to the Civil War when public schools were founded in communities across most of America outside the deep South, we would see traveling reformers, often members of state or trans-state associations, who linked up with local citizen leaders, churches, and voluntary membership groups. Regional networks of reformers and mobilized community groups worked together to found, shape, and sustain schools, usually one-room schools at first. This happened in virtually every village, town, and city neighborhood. Shared ideals and models communicated by traveling reformers gave public schools a certain similarity across America, but not because of any bureaucratic impositions from above. As historians of education David Tyack and Elisabeth Hansot sum up, the "mainstream of American public schooling during most of the nineteenth century was rural, chiefly unbureaucratic in structure, exhibiting only rudimentary professionalism, and dependent on the actions of hundreds of thousands of lay promoters and school trustees."[23]

Early U.S. social policies for mothers and children were championed by nationwide networks of women's associations, which also got involved in carrying through the programs once legislation was passed.[24] Launched in the 1870s, the Woman's Christian Temperance Union (WCTU) had some 7,000 locals in every U.S.

state by the turn of the century; and it became a pioneer in advocating not just laws prohibiting the sale of liquor but also many governmental and volunteer programs to aid mothers and children.[25] The General Federation of Women's Clubs (GFWC) was founded as a national organization in 1890; and by 1912 it boasted more than a million members spread across thousands of towns and cities in all the states and territories.[26] Federation groups agitated for the creation of the Children's Bureau and the Sheppard-Towner program; and they pressured dozens of state legislatures to pass protective labor laws for women, compulsory schooling laws, mothers' pensions, and many other measures for families and communities.

The National Congress of Mothers was also a leading force in nationwide campaigns for the Children's Bureau and mothers' pensions. The forerunner of the PTA, the National Congress was a federation of national, state, and local clubs launched in 1897 for the purpose of carrying "mother-love and mother-thought into all that concerns or touches childhood in Home, School, Church, State or Legislation."[27] Groups in the Mothers' Congress also joined local women's clubs of the General Federation in carrying through programs of the Children's Bureau, including efforts to collect statistics on infant mortality during the 1910s and efforts to set up local health clinics under Sheppard-Towner in the 1920s. The entire "maternalist era" in U.S. social policy making was marked by a remarkable partnership between female professionals working in the Children's Bureau in Washington, D.C., and voluntary associations of married women who were civically active in every community.

Tellingly, the women's associations active early in the twentieth century were membership-based but not strictly local. Women's groups in hundreds of towns and cities were connected to one another in a remarkable communication network with nationwide reach. Consequently, the women of the WCTU and the GFWC and the National Congress of Mothers/PTA had the ability to set statewide and nationwide agendas of public debate.

They mounted vivid moral arguments about the needs of mothers and children and the stake the nation had in helping them. By creating a sense of common agenda, and by persuading communities and states that they should compete with one another to pass good social programs, the women's federations countered, for a time, the usual tendency of U.S. subnational governments to engage in a "race to the bottom"—that is, to compete with one another to do less and less in the area of social programs. The women's groups of the early twentieth century could convincingly claim to speak to and for many local communities at once, and this made their messages convincing to politicians. They persuaded states to compete for priority in campaigns such as the enactment of mothers' pensions during the 1910s.

The Mothers' Congress and the General Federation worked closely with nationally prominent women professionals based in staff-led advocacy organizations. The National Consumers' League led by Florence Kelley is a good example, and so are many of the social settlement houses that existed in U.S. cities, each of which was staffed by reformist professionals and social workers who wanted governments to support new social programs for vulnerable groups. Interestingly, though, women professionals who created and used staff-led advocacy groups in the 1910s understood that they should not just talk with one another, and not just pressure the government in Washington or state capitals. (Female professionals understood this better than did male reformers of that time.) Women professionals who advocated for mothers and children through private groups such as the Consumers' League and the social settlement houses, and also the women professionals who staffed the federal Children's Bureau, made it a point to participate actively in the nationwide women's federations. They attended national, state, and local meetings with women who were married homemakers. And they sought to involve local groups of married women in civic projects and in crusades for new social legislation. In short, Progressive Era reformers like Jane Addams and Julia Lathrop did not simply talk

35

to their fellow professionals in Washington or New York City. They were actually out there in these grassroots federations, part of a national network of communication that could set priorities for simultaneous action.[28]

Landmark U.S. veterans' programs have also been nurtured by partnerships of widespread, locally rooted voluntary associations and government bureaus in Washington, D.C. By the 1880s, for example, the Grand Army of the Republic (GAR) had grown into the leading voluntary association of Union veterans. The GAR was a classic three-tiered voluntary civic association, with tens of thousands of local "posts" that met regularly, plus state and national affiliates that held big annual conventions. The GAR was open to Union veterans of all economic and ethnic backgrounds, including African Americans (who sometimes had their own posts, and sometimes attended the same posts as whites in states such as Massachusetts). The growth of the GAR was originally encouraged by the nascent Civil War benefits legislated between the 1860s and the early 1880s. In turn, the GAR spread the word about social programs, encouraging veterans to apply. The GAR monitored services and benefits for veterans and their survivors, to make sure these programs actually did what they were supposed to do. Of course the GAR pushed Congress to expand federal Civil War pensions; and GAR clout in northern Congressional districts helped assure that pension generosity would be sustained, even after fiscal conservatives started demanding cutbacks in this profligate (as they saw it) form of social spending.

This story was repeated for World War II veterans' benefits. In the 1940s, a nationwide veterans' association was already in existence. Founded right after World War I, the American Legion had over one million members by 1940, organized into more than 10,000 posts in cities and towns, and with "departments" in all of the states.[29] The Legion was an established power in Congressional lobbying and a force in the civic life of thousands of communities. In 1942, the Legion decided to recruit veterans returning from World War II, and turned its attention to shaping benefits and services for these young soldiers and their families. Without the Legion's ideas and political clout, the GI Bill would not have been as generous and democratically inclusive as it became.[30] The Legion drafted the bill that called for up to four years' worth of educational benefits and family allowances, as well as loans and employment assistance open to all returning veterans. The Legion was instrumental in persuading Congressional representatives, including skeptical Southern conservatives, to enact the very generous and comprehensive 1944 legislation. Thereafter, the American Legion and other veterans' associations worked closely with the Veterans Administration to administer the GI Bill and additional programs to assist veterans.

Social Security, finally, has a more complex relationship to voluntary associations. During the Great Depression when Social Security was launched, there was a militant social movement and voluntary federation of older Americans: The Townsend Movement, founded by a retired physician in Long Beach, California, spread across the country in the early 1930s, with thousands of local clubs and clout in many states.[31] Townsend clubs demanded that Congress pass a law allocating $200 a month (a huge sum at the time) to every older person, provided that he or she pledged to retire and spend the money right away to stimulate economic growth and employment for other Americans. This munificent plan horrified business leaders and most politicians. It certainly was not adopted. But it may have helped to spur Congress into creating the Social Security system of contributory retirement pensions; and Townsendites encouraged more generous expenditures on the elderly in a number of states.

The Townsend Movement fell apart by the late 1940s. Today, other seniors' organizations have grown up, above all the huge American Association of Retired Persons (AARP). As we shall see in Chapter Three, the AARP's growth over recent decades to encompass some 33 million Americans age fifty and older has been encouraged by generous federal social programs like Social

Security and Medicare, programs that the AARP currently monitors and strongly supports in Congress. Other old people's groups in many localities have also been stimulated by the growth of social provision for the elderly over the past four decades. The AARP, however, has only recently begun to nurture substantial numbers of regional and local membership chapters. If you talk to people in the AARP, they will tell you they recognize the need to develop stronger local organizational roots. As federal expenditures on benefits for the elderly come under greater and greater criticism, senior citizens are certainly politically aware citizens, because the newsletters and magazines of the AARP play a role in keeping elderly voters up to date on developments in Washington. But local AARP clubs could do much more to promote discussion among the elderly and between them and other citizens in communities and legislative districts across America. And if the AARP were based in local membership groups, rather than reaching individuals mainly via mailings, the AARP leadership would have an easier time understanding the needs and values of its constituents.

Backed by Reliable Public Revenues

The final characteristic of all successful U.S. social programs has been access to secure and growing sources of public funding. Both popular support and larger developments in the affairs of government have made this possible.

In a way, of course, access to public funds follows from the previous characteristics of successful social programs. If a social policy seems morally justified in the eyes of large numbers of Americans, if it enjoys a large cross-class constituency, and if it mobilizes voluntary groups, then that policy should fare well in decisions about the allocation of public resources. Public schools do well where many local groups are involved and supportive. Similarly, Civil War pensions and the GI Bill were supported by huge veterans' associations organized in thousands of local Congressional districts.[32] And the U.S. Children's Bureau benefited when letters and petitions from women's groups across the land urged Congress to increase appropriations for the Bureau and to pass the Sheppard-Towner Act of 1921.[33] Finally, as we all know, Social Security benefits have been virtually sacrosanct for many years in U.S. Congressional and presidential politics. So broad is the social support for Social Security and Medicare, and so vigilant are elder advocacy associations such as the AARP, that even in the 1990s Congressional representatives of either major party discuss cutbacks in those programs only at considerable political peril.

But generous and sustained government funding rests on more than just group clout or popularity with voters. Much depends on the robustness and dynamics of public finance, and the very particular kinds of tax revenues to which a social program becomes attached. What is happening to taxes in any given era is crucial, for if programs are not linked to reliable sources of funds they cannot readily deliver (or maintain) the sorts of generous benefits for cross-class constituencies that add up to political success in American democracy. Political support may lead to generous social spending, but it works the other way around, too.

Any social program launched with primarily local or state revenues can easily find itself subject to competition among subnational governmental entities to hold taxes down.[34] Arguably, U.S. public schools and welfare policies have always risked being starved for funds for this reason. However, a social program with a broad, cross-class constituency can still enjoy better access to local property taxes or various kinds of state revenues than a purely poverty program is likely to do. Public schools originally enjoyed such broad support in many local communities; and in any event, one-room primary schools, the first building blocks of the U.S. system, were not terribly expensive to run. In our day, suburban public schools enjoy very generous social and fiscal support from well-to-do and highly motivated parents. But public schools in impoverished cities and rural areas, as well as those in less-privileged suburbs, often face budgetary resistance from local

39

taxpayers, especially if most local residents are not parents of school-aged children. Older Americans are reluctant to increase tax-financed spending for public schools.[35] Residential segregation by race and class—and in some areas of the country, by age groups as well—can seriously undercut funding for public schools in all but the most affluent localities.

National-level social programs are likely to grow and sustain themselves over time only if they can tap into growing streams of public revenue.[36] Popular programs founded or expanded in the wake of major wars have tended to do best.

Civil War benefits could be so generously funded in the late nineteenth century in part because they were politically linked, via the hegemonic Republican Party of the day, to the chief revenue source for the federal government in that time: high tariffs on many industrial and agricultural goods.[37] Protective tariffs boosted the economic fortunes of key groups in the national Republican Party, and those same tariffs generated big budget "surpluses" for the federal treasury. Hard as it is to imagine from the perspective of late-twentieth-century U.S. politics, Republican Party politicians a century ago were not looking to cut taxes; they were looking for new, popular ways to spend burgeoning federal revenues. Pensions for millions of Union veterans and survivors were ideal expenditures, because they went disproportionately to Republican constituencies in the North, farmers and townspeople, who did not always benefit from the tariffs that the party also supported.[38] From the Civil War to World War I, in short, most Republicans, who represented states and Congressional districts outside the formerly Confederate South, benefited politically from a "benign circle" of taxing—through tariffs and spending—for Union veterans' benefits.

Maternalist social policies in early-twentieth-century America never succeeded as well in tapping into such a reinforcing tax-and-spend circle. They were limited in the public funding they could mobilize, and thus the benefits they could deliver to broad constituencies. During the 1910s, federated women's associations had considerable success at influencing public opinion and pressing dozens of state legislatures to enact mothers' pensions and protective labor laws for women. But the women's groups had a much harder time persuading localities and state legislatures to raise taxes to fund programs for mothers and children. This was an era of resistance to taxes by business groups and others concerned about the economic competitiveness of each state or locality, where funding decisions were made about mothers' pensions. At the federal level, meanwhile, tariffs were generating proportionately less revenue than they had in the late 1800s; and the federal income tax, instituted by a constitutional amendment in 1913, remained tiny until the 1940s, collecting modest revenues only from the wealthy.

The one maternalist social policy that managed to tap into expanded funding for a time was the milestone program I have highlighted, the Sheppard-Towner program of the early 1920s. This program offered federal subsidies for a set of services open not just to the poor but to all American mothers; consequently it was a popular program and women's groups were able to ally with the Children's Bureau to persuade Congress to increase the program's appropriations over its first years. But by the mid-1920s Sheppard-Towner had come under fierce attack from conservatives, including doctors who were opposed to federally supervised and financed health services. This happened just as women's federations were getting weaker and turning away from many of the political involvements they had taken on during the 1910s, and just as U.S. politicians figured out that newly enfranchised women voters were not likely to vote very differently than men. The original Sheppard-Towner legislation, enacted in 1921, had unfortunately not been structured as an open-ended entitlement. It was scheduled to expire in 1927 and had to be reauthorized by Congress. Although American women again raised their voice and majority support still existed in Congress, opponents in the Senate were able to use the institutional levers available to determined minorities to block reauthorization after 1929. Sheppard-Towner subsidies disappeared, and the Children's Bureau lost influence along with resources within the federal government.

U.S. federal government revenues expanded enormously in the wake of the New Deal and World War II.[39] During the 1930s, all levels of government were strapped for resources in a devastated economy, but the federal government gained relative leverage over local and state governments because of its continuing ability to borrow. Although the Roosevelt administration tried to cut taxes and reduce government spending, it also raised and deployed "emergency funding" to cover many economic and social programs. Then during World War II, the federal income tax was expanded to encompass much of the employed population.[40] Automatic payroll withholding was instituted, a device that makes tax payments less visible to citizens, thus ensuring a regular and expanding flow of revenues to the federal government during the postwar economic expansion.

Both the GI Bill of 1944 and the various programs enacted in the Social Security Act of 1935 benefited from the overall growth of federal revenues starting in the 1930s and 1940s. Yet Old Age Insurance—the part of the 1935 legislation that eventually became popular and virtually universal and usurped the label "Social Security"—carried its own source of funding: an earmarked payroll tax that was supposed to be used to build up a separate "trust fund" to cover future pension obligations. Because of President Roosevelt's fierce insistence on "fiscal soundness" for nonemergency social insurance programs, retirement insurance actually kicked in as a set of taxes well before any benefits were paid. After 1939, the program became more of a pay-as-you-go venture than originally planned.[41] Still, Social Security retirement insurance always benefited—ideologically as well as fiscally— from the existence of its earmarked payroll tax and nominally separate trust fund. Social Security taxes were deliberately labeled "contributions" and were treated as payments that built up individual "eligibility" for "earned benefits."[42]

As Social Security expanded to include more and more categories of employees, new taxes were collected ahead of the pay-
ment of benefits. Most retirees during the 1950s, 1960s, and
1970s actually did very well in terms of what they had paid into
the system over their working lives. Increasing Social Security
payroll taxes were accepted by the majority of American citizens as the system expanded toward near-universal coverage. And
once the coverage became very broad, the majority of citizens—
the elderly and their children—gained a stake in promised benefits. Even today, ordinary Americans do not object as much as one
might expect to Social Security taxes, despite their regressiveness
and the large cut they take from average incomes. Social Security's trust fund remains relatively solvent in an otherwise tight
federal budget; and ordinary Americans remain committed to
sustaining the system for the long run.

VEERING OFF COURSE

For a generation after World War II, U.S. social supports were
profoundly uneven across the races, since many African Americans, especially in the South, remained outside the core programs. Nevertheless, for a brief time, big and popular federal
programs—Social Security and the GI Bill—did a fair amount to
help young and old alike. These social programs cut across class
lines, were understood as returns for service to the community,
and were nurtured by associational support and rising tax revenues. But such prerequisites for social policy success started to
fall apart in the 1960s. Generational shifts and racial upheavals
help to explain why.

Social Provision for the Elderly Alone?

Spurred by the Great Depression and World War II, many
Western nations fashioned comprehensive welfare states to guar-
antee citizens full employment and social security.[43] In the
United States as well, New Deal reformers battled for broad pro-

tections for all citizens or wage earners. They fought for national jobs and unemployment insurance programs and tried to extend Social Security to include health insurance. Had reformers succeeded under Presidents Franklin Roosevelt and Harry Truman, the United States would have achieved its own version of a comprehensive welfare state. But liberal attempts were defeated in Congress, and by the 1950s the United States was left with only one permanent, broad-based social program—Social Security's contributory program of disability and retirement insurance. As other attempts to institutionalize broad social programs failed, America was set on the road to the missing middle in public social provision that pertains today.

True, gaps in social protection for the nonelderly were temporarily filled for many younger American families by the GI Bill of 1944 and subsequent federal veterans' legislation. Generous social investments in many young men and their families, coupled with hearty postwar economic expansion, ensured opportunity and security for millions of families. Especially well-served were those who entered the labor force, married, and raised children from the late 1940s into the 1960s.[44] But after that, the impact of the GI Bill waned, just as the American economy became much less rewarding for young workers and families.[45]

Another watershed for U.S. social policy came in the 1960s and early 1970s, when the War on Poverty, the Great Society, and many of the social policy initiatives of moderate Republican President Richard M. Nixon attempted to extend social benefits and training opportunities to poor people, including millions of African Americans, who had not been fully incorporated into the economic growth or social insurance protections of the postwar era.[46] But when the dust settled, the broadest and costliest national legislative achievements of the 1960s and 1970s focused on the elderly. The most important federal innovations were Medicare, enacted in 1965, and the indexing of Social Security pensions to inflation, which occurred in 1972. As sociologist Jill

Quadagno explains, "the 1972 amendments represented a turning point for Social Security, a watershed for U.S. welfare state development. The automatic cost-of-living increases removed benefits from politics and ensured older people that inflation would not erode the value of those benefits. . . . The 1972 amendments . . . solidly incorporated the middle class into the welfare state."[47] Most Americans, including the middle class, have since developed a strong stake in the benefits and protections of Social Security and Medicare.

Nowadays, the generational critiques and grand schemes for social policy reconstruction pushed by liberal and conservative advocates make sense in light of the generational imbalances that emerged in U.S. social provision after the 1960s. Gaps between generous and inclusive protections for the elderly and minimal supports for working-aged parents and their children are obvious now that the impact of the GI Bill has diminished. Although rhetoric changes from time to time, contemporary liberals and conservatives are carrying on old battles in new generational terms.

For example, the liberal advocate Marian Wright Edelman of the Children's Defense Fund got her start as a Civil Rights activist in the War on Poverty in Mississippi. When she moved to Washington, D.C., she turned to children's advocacy as the most promising approach for the 1970s and 1980s. As Edelman has explained, "support for whatever was labeled black and poor was shrinking and . . . new ways had to be found to articulate and respond to the continuing problems of poverty and race, ways that appealed to the self-interest as well as the conscience of the American people."[48] Funded by foundations and staffed by experts and lobbyists, the Children's Defense Fund appeals for social spending in the name of helping children and thus "investing" in our national future.

On the other side of the partisan spectrum, both conservative Republicans and fiscal watchdogs such as the Concord Coalition are looking for new ways to wean the American middle class from involvement with Social Security, Medicare, and other broad programs of public social provision. Conservatives, we should recall, have never liked Social Security (let alone its younger sibling Medicare). When Social Security was first becoming institutionalized between 1935 and the early 1950s, conservatives repeatedly tried to do away with the broad, contributory retirement insurance program launched by President Franklin Delano Roosevelt. Initially, conservatives criticized the assignment of individual Social Security numbers and tried to arouse voter resistance against new payroll taxes. Republican presidential contender Alf Landon raised these issues in 1936, but they went nowhere. Next, conservatives argued that the nation should immediately finance "more adequate" pensions to the very poor elderly alone, rather than trying to cover middle-class workers in a broad contributory program. Only in the 1950s did most Republicans finally give up and accept that Social Security, increasingly popular and inclusive, was here to stay—for a while, at least.

Why did conservatives originally argue against Social Security in the name of doing more for the poor? They understood that, especially in America, the only way to have a politically popular and fiscally healthy system of public pensions is to have the middle class included along with the poor. Conservatives did not want such a system, so they tried to keep the middle class out at the start. That original effort failed, but in recent decades conservatives have tried new tactics to take the middle class out of the Social Security system.

When Ronald Reagan achieved the presidency in 1980, fiscal conservatives hoped he would cut social spending on the middle class as well as programs for the very poor. But after briefly raising the possibility of such reforms, President Reagan and his budget director, David Stockman, quickly retreated from cutting middle-class programs in the face of an upsurge of public concern. Thereafter, the Reaganites concentrated rhetorical and budgetary fire on means-tested social spending for the poor.[49] At that point, in the mid-1980s, opponents of Social Security retreated to a more indirect and long-term effort to undermine middle-class faith in the Social Security system. Following tactics laid out in a remarkable article by Stuart Butler of the Heritage Foundation and Peter Germanis of the Cato Institute called "Achieving a Leninist Strategy," critics stopped calling for immediate cuts in Social Security and Medicare benefits, and instead began talking about a looming future "crisis" for the nation as a whole.[50]

Led in recent years by the Concord Coalition, fiscally conservative critics of Social Security stress the "injustice" of the payroll tax burden to younger workers, and suggest that working-aged taxpayers will eventually be crushed by the burden of paying pension and health care expenses for the large baby boom generation that will begin to retire after 2010. Cleverly, conservatives have targeted public opinion and sought to persuade younger Americans that Social Security will not be there when they eventually retire. According to conservatives, the future of the nation's economy and prospects for the young depend upon reducing taxes and expenditures for out-of-control retiree programs. Conservatives hope that Americans can be persuaded to rely on privately managed Wall Street investments to fund their retirements, leaving only the poor heavily reliant on public "safety nets." Once Social Security and Medicare are turned into residual welfare programs, they will be much easier to control— or trim—in the future.

Taking the middle class "off the dole" of Social Security and Medicare is thus the main goal of the Concord Coalition and its most visible national spokesman, investment banker Peter Peterson.[51] Meanwhile, conservative Republicans (including the erstwhile organizer of the 1994 Congressional victories, Newt Gingrich) are more careful about directly criticizing Social Security. Understanding how popular Social Security is with middle-class Americans, Republicans always say they want to "save" it—even when looking for ways to cut and restructure the shared features of the system.

Congressional Republicans aim above all to extend the "Reagan Revolution" as a tax-cutting enterprise. Balancing the federal budget is a primary goal for the Concord Coalition, but not for most conservative Republicans. Certainly, budget balance is not an aim to be pursued through tax increases of any kind. Rather, calls for fiscal responsibility by most contemporary Republicans are meant to gain middle-class support for shrinking the federal government—and cutting taxes on the wealthy along the way.

Generational imbalances in social policy have, in sum, opened the door to today's national preoccupations with old versus young, and to the contemporary debate about the scope of public social provision. Advocacy groups and partisan politicians structure public debates around the sharp imbalance between America's relatively generous and comprehensive retirement programs, versus the paltry efforts to help only a minority of nonelderly adults and children. Even if most citizens instinctively shy away from actual "generational warfare," the imbalances of social protections by age group really are there; and so advocacy arguments gain some resonance with real-life experience.

But why have budget-balancers and tax-cutters made so much headway in recent arguments about the future of American social provision, while liberal child advocates often maneuver for adjustments around the edges? Why isn't there a powerful social and political movement in the field arguing for America to do more through the federal government to support working families in general? After all, an obvious way to respond to inherited generational imbalances in U.S. social provision since the fading of the GI Bill would be to find new ways to renew and enhance the nation's commitment to young families. We could enact universal health insurance and strong supports for working families. We need not respond to current generational imbalances by cutting off the elderly, too.

Logical as a broader approach might be in America today, recent political transformations have undermined each of the four sets of conditions for successful social policy making in American democracy. Anyone who would like to revitalize the long-standing tradition best exemplified in recent times by the Social Security Act and the GI Bill needs to have a clear picture of what has gone wrong over the past generation.

The Failure of a Dream

Imagine what might have happened after African Americans finally achieved basic civil rights between 1955 and 1965. As blacks finally won the right to vote, the United States at last became a kind of democracy for everyone, not just for whites. Briefly in the mid-1960s, liberal Democrats gained executive power and majorities in Congress; and some dreamed of "completing" the social and economic agendas left over from the unfinished New Deal reforms of the 1930s and 1940s. Active full-employment programs might have been designed—to make sure that every American adult could get job training and a job with wages and benefits sufficient to support a family. Such employment programs would have aided the poor along with other Americans, offering help to all nonelderly adults willing to serve the nation through work. Progressives in the 1960s might also have fashioned new security programs such as universal health coverage—a social benefit that is vital for any family trying to raise children.

But this dream did not come true. In the immediate aftermath of the Civil Rights struggles in the South, it proved impossible to unite unions and Civil Rights activists (despite efforts by leaders like Walter Reuther, Bayard Rustin, and Martin Luther King). National-level policy making went forward in already well-worn grooves. Institutional and policy legacies from the New Deal era encouraged policy makers to model Medicare on Social Security, thus restricting universal health coverage to the elderly alone.[52] Existing patterns of macroeconomic management encouraged the Kennedy and Johnson administrations to use "commercial Keynesian" tax cuts to stimulate the national economy.[53] Tiny job training programs and targeted welfare efforts were what remained to help the very poor. Between the mid-1960s and mid-1970s, millions of needy single-parent families were added to the welfare rolls, becoming eligible as well for Medicaid and other means-tested assistance.[54] This helped a lot of very poor mothers and children, but left millions of other poor and less-privileged families out in the cold.

A fierce political backlash soon gathered force.[55] As many Americans faced declining economic prospects from the early 1970s, and as more and more women entered the wage-labor force by choice or necessity, welfare programs targeted on some very poor mothers (stereotyped as black) could easily be portrayed as unfair. Conservatives played this theme for all it was worth. And many ordinary Americans responded. It has hardly mattered that, just to survive, most welfare mothers on AFDC (Aid to Families with Dependent Children) had to work part-time off the books.[56] The point is more cultural and political: AFDC benefits originally conceived as "mothers' pensions" lost their legitimacy in an era of racial conflict, declining wages, and widespread female entry into the wage-labor market.

For more than a generation, welfare served as a spectacularly successful conservative political battering ram against "liberals." Republican President Nixon expanded welfare benefits (as well as affirmative action), then turned around and criticized these policies to spark conflicts among Democrats. Ronald Reagan featured antiwelfare appeals as part of his winning campaign for the presidency in 1980. Intellectual and political attacks on welfare subsequently deepened and spread to Democrats—culminating in the bipartisan Congressional majorities that voted to "end welfare as we know it" in August 1996. In U.S. politics it has always been difficult to justify social benefits for the poor alone; and never more so than in recent decades.

Liberal Democrats, in short, missed opportunities and worked themselves into a political impasse. As the effects of the GI Bill faded, two crucial tenets of the long-standing formula for successful American social provision—giving support to people across classes, and justifying social benefits as supports for recipients seen as "contributors" to the community—were *not* extended to new social programs for the nonelderly. Welfare programs proliferated instead, but soon became racially controversial and culturally delegitimated in an era of changing roles for women. After the 1960s, nobody in the Democratic base was happy. Welfare efforts failed to reverse economic and family trends that meant poverty for more and more families, while millions of downscale Americans were left without forms of assistance (such as Medicaid) that were available to some of the very poor.[57]

Here was simply an untenable situation for Democrats: They came to be seen as champions of ineffectual poverty programs—rather than as advocates of opportunity and security for all families. Republicans, meanwhile, turned more and more toward racially divisive political maneuvers and toward efforts to shrink government and cut taxes on the rich. No one, it has seemed, is able to speak up on behalf of a social politics that would benefit the less privileged while bringing most Americans together.

A Transformed Political Universe

Partnerships between voluntary membership associations and government constituted another long-standing ingredient of successful U.S. social policy making. In this respect, it would seem at first glance that conditions since the 1960s should have become more rather than less conducive to successful social policy making. After all, policy advocacy groups have proliferated at a remarkable rate in U.S. democracy.[58] Thousands of them, spanning all parts of the political spectrum, have set up headquarters in Washington, the better to pressure Congress to enact or amend legislation, and the better to monitor federal agencies as they implement regulations or subsidies or spending programs.[59] Although many of the advocacy groups that have proliferated in recent decades are trade and business associations, this is by no means the case universally. Lots of "citizens'" groups emerged from the 1960s onward, including some groups advocating for the poor, such as the Children's Defense Fund.[60] It is also true that many federal, state, and local social services for the poor are jointly administered through private associations, such as the Salvation Army or Catholic Charities; and such associations are in turn active in lobbying governments about matters of concern to them and their clients.

As new civic associations have multiplied since the 1960s, membership federations of the kind once central to American civic life and social policy making have waned. And most of the recently created advocacy groups are professionally led, Washington-based organizations that relate to their individual members by sending them computer-generated mailings of letters, magazines, or newsletters, and asking members to send checks in return.[61] Contemporary advocacy groups usually do not have large memberships or regular local and state group activities. Until recently, for example, an advocacy group such as the Children's Defense Fund had little organizational presence outside of Washington. It depended on mailings, media coverage, and moral exhortation to get across its message. Unfortunately, for all that the CDF has a compelling cause, a charismatic leader (Marian Wright Edelman), and substantial funding from foundations and corporations, it cannot equal the resources for influencing the media and public opinion that antigovernment advocacy groups can muster. The CDF has had trouble engaging in popular mobilization or responding to popular concerns at the grassroots level. CDF "members" have been names on a mailing list of modest length, and most of those who come to its annual conferences are social service professionals. (Recognizing these limitations, the CDF is currently working to stimulate a network of dispersed and locally rooted membership groups.)

Even when today's staff-led advocacy groups are very large—a good example is the American Association of Retired Persons, with over 33 million names on its dues-paying mailing lists—they tend not to have strong social roots in local communities or in the fifty states. The AARP certainly has a vast communications network that reaches older American households everywhere. In that sense the AARP has much more clout than the Children's Defense Fund—and Congress knows it! But even the AARP has only modest capacities to understand and guide public opinion.

Today's top-heavy, Washington-oriented advocacy groups stand in sharp contrast to the great historic voluntary federations—such as the Grand Army of the Republic; the National Congress of Mothers and General Federation of Women's Clubs; the Townsend Movement; and the American Legion—that helped to bring about and perhaps sustain the broadest social policies in America's past. Those federations were not only large in terms of individual dues-paying members; they were also organizationally rooted in regular local face-to-face meetings, and they had elected leaderships in each state as well as at the national level. The traditional broad voluntary associations of American democracy crossed class lines, brought community-based groups together, *and* created bridges across towns and cities and across regions. To be sure, they were very influential with Congress in the nation's capital, but their influence was rooted in what they did in and across local legislative districts. These great historic federations tended to be sensitive to local community opinion. If their average members wanted or believed something, they took those values and ideas as their cue when proposing new legislation or seeking to influence the way governments carried out existing laws.

Even as top-down, professionally led, and Washington-centered advocacy groups have become more prevalent and active in U.S. politics at the relative expense of locally rooted membership groups, parallel changes have occurred in the political party and electoral systems. Since the advent of television advertising, computerized mailing lists, and continuous polling, U.S. electoral politics has been an increasingly top-down affair. The local organizational roots of political parties have atrophied, espe-

53

cially on the Democratic side of the spectrum, where both trade unions and local political machines have declined. Contributions of money count for more and more in U.S. politics, while contributions of time and effort weigh less heavily.[62] Meanwhile, aspiring politicians hold fund-raisers among privileged business and professional people, in order to raise the huge funds needed to hire pollsters and consultants. These professionals, in turn, treat citizens as subjects of polls or focus groups. They gather data to identify small groups of swing voters, who then can be bombarded with emotional media messages leading into election day.[63] Fewer and fewer voters are likely to be directly contacted by politicians or party activists.[64] A clear-cut exception is on the right of the political spectrum, where the Christian Coalition has managed to link evangelical church congregations and local political clubs to local and state Republican parties in about one-third of the states.[65]

Overall, however, changes in electoral and party politics since the 1950s go hand in hand with changes in the voluntary group universe. Except for Christian Coalition members—along with some AFL-CIO union members, and retirees in places with senior citizens' groups in touch with elder advocacy groups—most Americans today are not likely to be involved in locally rooted yet nationally influential associations with a direct stake in current social policy making. They are not likely personally to be members of local political clubs, union halls, or local branches of fraternal, women's, or civic groups that weigh in on social policy debates in Washington and state capitals. And they are not likely to have family members, friends, or neighbors who are active in such groups. This situation helps make sense of the "missing middle" in U.S. social policy debates. For today's debates are mostly shaped by elites—business leaders, professionals, pollsters, media chieftains, and politicians—who are not in touch with, counterbalanced by, or accountable to grassroots groups of citizens in communities across the land.

The GI Bill of 1944, for example, would have turned out very differently if the American Legion of that day had not written the legislation and shaped the debate—or if the Legion had been principally a bunch of professionals and pollsters in Washington. The 1940s American Legion had local roots in communities all across the United States, which made it sensitive to the many needs of a broad array of veterans. The Legion used its clout across virtually all U.S. Congressional districts to push for legislation that delivered generous and comprehensive benefits. If, instead, the drafting and enactment of the GI Bill had been left entirely in the hands of the elites of that time—whether they were the liberal New Dealers, the established university educators, or conservative Congressional representatives—the resulting legislation would have offered much more limited educational and economic benefits to only some, not all, of the returning World War II veterans.[66]

Although the American Legion was, on the face of it, a "conservative" group, its three-tiered structure and its popular membership roots made a big difference for the development of one of the most comprehensive U.S. social programs. The absence—or dwindling strength—of such membership associations today means that initiatives like the GI Bill are hard to repeat, because conservative and liberal elites can always figure out ways to limit government programs to marginal constituencies.

Budget Stringency and Eroding Taxes

The final aspect of successful U.S. social policy making is access to reliable public revenues. But this, too, has become imperiled in recent decades. We have noted the resistance to tax paying that Republicans and other conservatives helped to encourage in the wake of the Great Society. In addition, major federal tax cuts were enacted in 1981, leading to a burgeoning federal deficit that made it virtually impossible for new social programs to be funded during the late 1980s and most of the 1990s.[67]

The Reagan ascendancy of the 1980s did not at first eliminate many social programs or cut absolute domestic social spending, but it did retard the growth of expenditures on targeted programs that had already lost considerable ground in the face of inflation during the 1970s. More important, the Reagan era signaled an ideological sea change.[68] Both politicians' rhetoric, and the actual squeezing and disrupting of governmental programs that occurred in this period, helped to delegitimate governmental responses to domestic social ills. Politicians became reluctant to discuss taxation as a positive means to the resolution of civic or individual concerns. And the huge federal budget deficit created by Ronald Reagan's tax cuts itself moved to the center of public discussion as supposedly the leading problem for the nation to resolve in the 1990s—neatly directing attention away from the increasingly acute difficulties faced by less-educated working families in the national economy.

Taxes are arguably the pivot on which the future of federal social policy may turn. Conservatives today are determined to severely cut both federal taxes and future public social spending. The real aim is to shift U.S. savings into private investment funds. Antigovernment forces appeal to American middle-class citizens as taxpayers—especially as payers of property and income taxes—rather than as potential beneficiaries of existing or new broadly focused social programs. Making discussion of new (or even sustained) taxes unthinkable is an important part of the contemporary conservative political agenda.

Antigovernment conservatives are hard at work trying to reduce American middle-class faith in the viability and legitimacy of "middle-class entitlements" such as Social Security and Medicare. Conservatives who are opposed to large governmental programs understand well that these programs will be hard to cut back as long as they enjoy middle-class support. And taxes cannot be slashed if Americans want them to pay for Social Security and Medicare (or other broadly popular social programs). It is therefore not incidental that contemporary conservative tactics for shrinking Social Security and Medicare take the form of efforts to convince young middle-class employees that these universal programs are a "bad deal" for them, while simultaneously suggesting that first Medicare and then Social Security are "bound to go bankrupt" as the baby boom generation ages. If younger middle-class Americans can be taken out of Medicare and Social Security as taxpayers and potential beneficiaries, then retirement investments can be shifted into the private financial sector. What is more, U.S. political history suggests that without full middle-class participation, Medicare and Social Security would become "welfare" programs for the poor. It would then be politically easy to cut these programs again and again in the future.

On the other side of the political spectrum, progressives want to increase governmentally funded "investments" not only in the economy, but also in education, health care, and other social services. Progressives have already lost many battles to expand substantially such social programs to the degree that they are narrowly targeted on the poor, on blacks, or on inner cities. Liberals are still trying to expand targeted programs for children.

But many members of the U.S. voting public are either relatively indifferent to children's programs, especially when they are targeted on the poor, or else are suspicious that such measures are a proxy for "welfare" expenditures or make-work social service jobs.[69] One way out for progressives is to advocate, as the early Clinton administration did, either tax subsidies for the less privileged or extensions of universal "security" programs—such as "health care for all"—to aid the middle class as well as the poor. Yet such progressive strategies are badly hampered by the unwillingness of U.S. politicians today, including many Democrats, to talk publicly about the raising of revenues to finance broad social programs. After all, tax breaks can hardly be added indefinitely as a tool of federal social policy in an era of tight budgets and restricted revenues. And broad new social programs—like health care for all—cannot happen unless they have nationally channeled resources behind them.[70]

Looking to the Future

There is, in sum, no escaping the need to consider social policies in relation to sources of public revenue. In the future, as well as in the past, successful social policies will have to be linked to well-accepted and sufficient sources of revenue. As we proceed in this book, we will consider taxes as well as social policies. For the two go together. We will also consider whether existing social protections for the elderly can be reformed, and new, more adequate social supports for young families devised, in ways that recapitulate historic formulas for social policy success in the United States.

Again and again Americans have banded together to support, and benefit from, governmentally administered social programs that really have helped large numbers of citizens become full contributors to the national community. In recent decades, this formula for successful social policy making in American democracy has faded from view. But it may not be too late to try it again, to address today's issues for the old, the young, for all of us together.

CHAPTER THREE   *The Uneasy Security of Our Grandparents*

LOUISE W_____, age 73, lives by herself in a single fur-
nished room on the third floor of a rooming house located in a
substandard section of the city. In this one room, she cooks, eats
and sleeps. . . . Widowed at 64, she has few friends remaining
from her younger years. . . . [S]he stays confined to her one room
and the bathroom shared by nine other people. When the
weather is warm enough, she ventures down the long flight of
stairs about once a week for a walk to the corner and back.[1]

"Louise W" was featured in *The Other America: Poverty in the
United States*, the influential 1962 exposé by Michael Harrington
that helped to spur the federal antipoverty efforts of the 1960s
and early 1970s. Ironically entitled "The Golden Years," Chapter
6 of Harrington's passionate book probed the plight of the nearly
"fifty percent of the elderly" who then existed "below minimum
standards of decency."[2] Difficult as it is to picture now, four
decades ago elderly Americans were more likely to be poor than
their younger fellow citizens.

Many of the elderly in 1960 had never enjoyed good incomes,
so the "misery of their old age" was "simply the conclusion of a
life of misery."[3] But others had drifted "down from a working life
of decent wages to an old age of dependency and social workers."[4]
That so much deprivation for the elderly should occur in the

59

world's richest nation, Harrington attributed chiefly to an ungenerous and "upside-down" U.S. welfare state. Social Security payments, he wrote, were often "completely inadequate to a decent life."[5] Public "relief," if available at all in any given state or locality, was accompanied by demeaning means tests and bureaucratic hassles.[6]

Private sector protections were not adequate either. Extended family ties had attenuated and the 1950s elderly got only about 10 percent of their income from other family members, with most such help going to the better-off.[7] "Individual charity and private pension plans account for only a fraction of the needs of these people," Harrington noted.[8] In the absence of national health insurance the unavailability of affordable private insurance coverage was especially grievous. Rapidly rising costs for doctors and hospitals had "priced the care of the aged out of the budget of millions of American families."[9]

"The brochure writers and the publicists talk of the 'golden years' and of 'senior citizens,'" Harrington bitterly concluded in 1962. "But these are euphemisms to ease the conscience of the callous. America tends to make its people miserable when they become old, and there are not enough phrases in the dictionary to gloss over this ugly reality."[10]

How startling has been the change in the image of older Americans since these biting words were penned. "The golden years" now seems an apt, not bitterly ironic, description. Happy, healthy faces of retired men and women stare out at us from ads on television, in magazines, on billboards. *Modern Maturity*—the monthly magazine sent to the more than 33 million Americans fifty years and over who are on the rolls of the American Association of Retired Persons (AARP)—is full of ads and feature stories about vacations, hobbies, engaging "second careers," and appealing volunteer activities. Discounts for "senior citizens" are advertised everywhere—on buses and subways, at motels, in America's national parks, at stores and restaurants. The elderly

are an enticing market opportunity for businesses; and governments also lavish benefits and privileges upon them. A popular
guidebook tells Americans about *Unbelievably Good Deals and
Great Adventures That You Absolutely Can't Get Unless You're
Over 50.*[11]

All of this both dignifies the elderly and glamorizes retirement
as a stage of life. Nowadays, in fact, more than three-quarters of
American women and two-thirds of men retire as soon as possible, and people who make this move between ages fifty-five and
sixty-two are "about as likely to say they retired because they
wanted to as to cite conventional health reasons."[12] Back in the
1950s, Americans looked upon the prospect of retirement with
ambivalence at best. Legally enforced by employers, retirement
brought a possible sense of "uselessness, irresponsibility, and inadequacy" along with the very real possibility of "a late-life descent
into economic insecurity."[13] "These concerns seem quaintly irrelevant" in the 1990s, observe demographers Judith Treas and
Ramon Torrecilha. "No longer faintly distasteful, retirement,
especially early retirement, has become a centerpiece of the
American dream. . . . Older Americans have embraced retirement and, when they do work, work at part-time jobs."[14]

But the "golden" appellation also has a more sinister connota-
tion in contemporary portrayals of the elderly. Since the mid-
1980s, opinion leaders and editorialists in the highbrow media
have taken to portraying oldsters as overly privileged and a burden on the young. Media accounts present wealthy-looking
retirees standing around on lush golf courses, spending the proceeds from Social Security checks funded from exorbitant taxes
collected from hard-pressed young workers. We Americans "Soak
the Young to Enrich the Old" according to the headline on a
1986 commentary in the *Washington Post*.[15] The United States
has a "Welfare State for the Affluent," which "allocates most benefits on the basis of seniority alone. . . . [M]ore than 60 percent of
all federal benefit spending flows to the 12 percent of Americans who are age sixty-five or older."[16] "Today's elderly are bring-

ing down the social welfare state and threatening the nation's economic future," agrees Lester Thurow writing in a May 1996 issue of the *New York Times Magazine*.[17] The striking cover of a September 1995 "MediScare" issue of *Newsweek* portrays a young man holding aloft an old lady in a wheelchair, with the bold-lettered query "Young vs. Old: Who Will Carry the Burden?"[18]

Not just young adults but innocent children are portrayed as victims of the greedy elderly. "Are Kids Shortchanged as Seniors Reap Vast Federal Benefits?," rhetorically queries a 1995 commentary in *Business Week*.[19] The answer turns out to be yes, of course. As the headline on the commentary indicates, the youngest Americans at the end of the twentieth century are "Victims of the Golden Years," and it is only going to get worse in the next century, as the post–World War II baby boomers head off to those golf courses.

"Gray Power!" is said to be the reason for such elderly privilege in contemporary America. Or so we learn from a 1988 *Time* magazine special on how the AARP has emerged "as the nation's most powerful special-interest lobby."[20] Far from being socially marginal and politically powerless as Michael Harrington portrayed them in 1962, the U.S. elderly today are often viewed as omnipotent. Along with dozens of other advocacy organizations, the elderly have a powerful lobbying giant, the AARP, with tens of millions of enrolled members, a huge annual budget, and a magnificent headquarters building that possesses its own zip code in Washington. Observers often underline that the AARP is second in size only to the Catholic Church. As voters and as lobbyists, the American elderly are supposedly an irresistible political force, before which grown Congressional representatives invariably quiver in fear or deference. "Think of the American Association of Retired Persons as grandfather, very big and very rich," writes Lee Smith in *Fortune* magazine. "When grandfather taps his knife on the water glass, . . . everyone at the table pays attention. It could be the start of an expensive project, and everyone else might have to give up at least a second helping of dinner."[21]

During the final decades of the twentieth century, in short, the image of the American elderly has taken a startling turn. Not so long ago people in their sixties and older were seen as pitiable, poor, and politically weak. Now they are often portrayed as privileged and exceedingly powerful—to the point of greediness. Oldsters in America today are much to be envied, it seems—especially by their children and grandchildren who, according to many pundits, are paying mounting bills to support government benefits to let retirees live lives of affluence and leisure.

What are we to make of such a sudden transformation of social imagery? Are today's older Americans really so much better off than their counterparts were in the 1950s and 1960s? To the degree that many of the U.S. elderly are doing better, why has this happened? What role have public policies played, compared to demographic and economic trends? And what about the political power of the elderly? Are elderly voters and advocacy groups responsible for the present—and likely future—shape of U.S. social provision? This chapter addresses these questions, before concluding with a brief look at the dilemmas to be addressed as America and its aging population move into a new century.

In truth, most of America's grandparents *have* achieved a considerable new modicum of economic security in recent decades. This has been a triumphant achievement for American social policy at its best, because relatively generous and inclusive public programs—chiefly Social Security and Medicare—deserve much of the credit for turning around the situation of our grandparents. As their lives have become economically secure, older Americans have also become more civically engaged.

But mere "Gray Power" did not bring about national supports for retirees. America's social programs for the elderly have enjoyed broad political support from citizens of all age groups. Families of modest means have an enormous stake in maintaining, even enhancing, these programs. Here is one realm of American social policy where the middle has not been missing—and the only question is whether responsiveness to the values and needs of regular working families will continue in an era of conservative counterattacks against the inclusive and shared features of social provision for the elderly.

RISING FORTUNES AND PERSISTENT INSECURITIES

Contemporary images of happy, comfortable elders have a basis in economic and social reality, because recent times have been unprecedentedly good for Americans sixty-five years and older. Good fortunes for the elderly in general are apparent in all of the ways that would seem to matter most: life and health; independent living; wealth and income security. At the same time, pockets of often extreme poverty and isolation remain—especially for nonwhites and very old women living by themselves. We need to look at both the bright spots and the dark areas of the picture.

Health and Prosperity

Back at the start of the twentieth century, people sixty-five and older accounted for only one out of twenty-five Americans, but now they are one-eighth of the national population, and the proportion of elderly will rise to one-fifth in the middle decades of the twenty-first century. Of course the elderly have become a bigger share of the population in part because Americans are having fewer children per family than they did a century ago. But people are also living a lot longer. Life expectancy for those who made it as far as sixty years increased significantly during the 1970s and 1980s. Millions now live into their eighties and beyond.

Heart disease is the leading cause of death for adults, but after 1968 the United States made rapid medical progress in preventing and treating such disease.[22] Of course, chronic disabilities are becoming more problematic, as more and more Americans live not just to become "old" (as gerontologists call those beyond age sixty-four), but also to become "old-old" (after seventy-four), or to join the ranks of the "oldest old" (beyond age eighty-four). Persistent ailments such as arthritis, hypertension, and cataracts take hold as people age, and these conditions can make prolonged life unpleasant.[23] Still, in recent years, U.S. medicine has made remarkable strides in mitigating many such chronic conditions, too. And more progress can be expected.

In a number of respects older Americans report following better personal-health practices than do adults under sixty-five.[24] And seniors today perceive themselves to be reasonably healthy. According to a 1989 survey of older Americans living in the community (that is, not in nursing homes), more than 70 percent reported that their health was "excellent," "very good," or "good" compared with others of their age.[25] Three-generation vacations are becoming increasingly common in the United States, noted a July 1996 *New York Times* article called "Holiday Travelers Make Room for Grandma."[26] Grown children and grandchildren now spend many years of life in the company of healthy grandparents, who are able to travel and participate in other active pursuits with their loved ones.

Older Americans often feel well enough to continue working part-time, too. Some badly need the extra income, while others continue to work at least part-time by choice rather than from sheer necessity. In 1990 as in 1980, the average age of retirement continued to be sixty-four, compared to sixty-nine as it was in 1950. Since the 1980 census, however, there has been a modest increase in labor-force participation for elderly men, most of it in part-time jobs.[27] Mandatory retirement was abolished by law between 1978 and 1986, and the U.S. economy has generated more part-time employment in recent years. Retired people can earn modest amounts without losing Social Security benefits; and they can continue to rely on Medicare. "Ironically," note Treas and Torrecilha, "the economic restructuring that has fostered part-time jobs, temporary employment, and the use of low-wage contractors to supply parts or perform services has served the needs of older people, even while undermining the economic security of younger workers."[28]

Retired people in the United States value living independently as owners or renters, so it is significant that "older Americans became more likely during the 1980s to keep their own homes and less likely to live in the households of kin."[29] In 1990, a whopping 91 percent of men sixty-five years and older, and 84 percent of women, were either householders or spouses of householders. Only one in twenty of the elderly (mostly very old women) lived in nursing homes. Rates of residential independence for America's seniors went up remarkably between 1950 and 1990, increasing 17 percent for men and 30 percent for women. There are various reasons for this, including the declining incidence of widowhood and general increases in elder income security.

Also important is the advantage that Americans who have become elderly in the late 1980s and early 1990s previously enjoyed in the national housing market. They were young adults soon after World War II, and thus many were aided by low-cost mortgages, an expanding housing stock, and reasonable housing prices in the 1950s and 1960s, followed by sharp appreciation of the price of earlier housing investments in the 1970s and 1980s.[30] In 1990, more elderly Americans were likely to own their own homes than was the case for the elderly in 1980; and elderly Americans enjoyed a discernible ownership advantage in comparison to younger adults.

Economic security for older Americans also reached an unprecedentedly positive level during the 1980s. Part of the reason has to do with the value of homes that many people owned as they reached retirement, because home ownership is the principal source of wealth for most Americans who hold any significant assets at all. Home equity accounts for only about one-quarter of the net assets all Americans hold, however, and during the mid-1980s people over age sixty-nine made significantly greater strides in overall wealth ownership than did younger age groups.[31] By 1988, about 40 percent of the net worth of elderly households was in home equity; another 30 percent was in savings and checking accounts; and the rest was in financial investments, real estate, and shares of businesses or professions.[32]

Wealth aside, most elderly Americans now enjoy at least minimally decent incomes. Since the 1950s, older American adults, who are more and more likely to have stopped working for wages, have nevertheless steadily improved their income status compared to younger working-aged adults.[33] "Median" incomes are the best measure here, for they are the incomes made by people right in the middle of the full income distribution. Measurements adjusted for family sizes and needs show that from 1949 on, median-income gains for families headed by elderly persons steadily fared better than median-income gains for all Americans, with especially sharp increases in elderly median income occurring during the period between 1973 and 1991. During that time the median adjusted income of elderly families went up by 34 percent, while median-income gains for all persons went up by only 10.6 percent.[34]

No matter how trends are measured, poverty among the U.S. elderly has plummeted in recent decades. Michael Harrington was correct to dramatize elderly poverty in *The Other America*. He spoke of severe economic want for about half of the elderly in 1960, no doubt grouping together those below the official U.S. poverty line and many others hovering very near it in the late 1950s and early 1960s. Even by the strict official U.S. poverty measures that the Bureau of the Census calculated from 1959 onward, more than a third of the elderly remained poor in 1960 and nearly a quarter were still poor in 1970. By 1996, however, the elderly poverty rate had dropped to 10.8 percent, nearly 3 points below the overall U.S. poverty rate of 13.7 percent.

For most of modern history, the elderly were considerably more likely to be poor than younger Americans. During the era between the end of World War II and the late 1960s, poverty declined for everyone in a growing national economy. But the elderly still struggled with economic deprivation more often than younger Americans. During the last twenty-five years, however, something quite new has happened. Elderly Americans have gained ground economically relative to working-aged adults and —especially—in comparison to children. The rising U.S. child poverty rate crossed the declining elder poverty rate around 1974, and by now America's elderly are only about half as likely to live in poverty as America's children, a fifth of whom are poor. Poverty for the elderly is now close to the rate for adults in general—including childless adults, who do better economically than parents who are responsible for children. A startling generational turnaround has occurred.

The Other Elderly Americans

There is, in short, some truth in the shifting imageries noted at the start of this chapter. Seniors in the United States *are* doing better than ever before, especially in the ways we can measure with economic information. Projections of the same kinds of information tell us that, for the next decade or so, Americans arriving at old age will continue to do fairly well economically, as new waves of people reach retirement with more wealth than their immediate predecessors, and with at least comparable pension benefits.

But statistics that lump huge numbers of older Americans together can be partially misleading. Averages and general trends tell us little about the disparate fortunes of particular subgroups within the ranks of the elderly. While many older Americans are comfortable—and a fraction are unprecedentedly wealthy— many others remain (or will become over time) very poor. Indeed, large numbers of older Americans find themselves hovering precariously close to acute neediness, even if they have not yet slipped below any official "poverty line."

To discuss income differences among today's U.S. elderly, our sociological experts Judith Treas and Ramon Torrecilha point to four groupings. As they put it: "The *poor* have incomes below the government poverty line; the *near-poor* have incomes that lift them no more than 150 percent above the poverty line. Those we call *comfortable* have incomes exceeding their poverty line by five times or more. Falling between the near-poor and the comfortable are *middle*-income elderly."[35] Just over half (54 percent) of the American elderly fall into the middle-income category. Less than one-fifth are "comfortable" (and only some of these can be labeled truly wealthy). At the other end of the scale, 27 percent of the elderly fall into the "poor" and "near-poor" categories combined—significantly more than are found in the "comfortable" groups. What is more, larger numbers of elderly than nonelderly Americans hover near the poverty line, so that the totals below 150 percent of poverty are significantly greater for older Americans.[36]

In short, the big change since the time of Michael Harrington's classic book has been to move the bulk of America's elderly from real want toward a middling level of material well-being (where people enjoy incomes clearly above the poverty line). This is indeed a huge transformation, and one worth celebrating. But it would not be fair at all to conclude that most older Americans are living in luxury. Consumption measures confirm that older people are not, for the most part, free-spending "rich uncles." In general, elderly households have less cash income and consume less per person than younger households. Older people spend more of their consumption dollars on "essentials" such as housing, food, and medical care than do Americans in younger households.[37]

As any reader might guess, different kinds of older people fare unequally. Whites are better off than blacks and Hispanics; and elderly people with more education do better than those with less.[38] The most telling contrasts are based on gender as well as race, and on how long people live and whether they are married or living alone. More than four out of five elderly men enjoy incomes putting them in either the "comfortable" or the "middle" category, while almost a third of elderly women are likely to be poor or near-poor.

Widowed women are especially likely to be poor, as are women living alone—and naturally these are often the same people, because a widowed woman probably will live alone. As of the last census the poverty rate for black women living alone was an astounding 60.6 percent. Within this doleful category were many of the needy and isolated old people who died during a 1995 summer heat wave in Chicago, locked in their apartments and afraid to go out for fear of attacks on their persons or their property by criminals.[39] The next summer, in 1996, more old people living alone died in overheated Midwestern cities like Oklahoma City, reportedly because they feared to spend what it would cost to run their air conditioners.[40]

Older American men tend to benefit from diversified sources of income. They get about 30 percent of their income from Social Security; 23 percent from investments like stocks or bonds; 25 percent from wages for (perhaps part-time) employment; and the final 19 percent from private pensions.[41] Older women, by contrast, do not enjoy such a rich and diversified array of sources of income. Overall, 44 percent of the income of older women comes from Social Security. And very old, poor women are even more totally dependent on public benefits. Journalist Lisa Genasci succinctly summarizes the female predicament:

> Because they've tended to be homemakers, sporadic participants in the work force or employees predominantly in lower-wage jobs, many women are losing out in company sponsored pension plans. For the same reasons, their Social Security checks are significantly lower than men's, and many have little or no savings.[42]

Especially for women who are widowed, Social Security survivor benefits alone, even if supplemented by Supplemental Security Income and food stamps, may not be enough to keep them out of poverty, or far from it.

Ironically, older men benefit in some ways by dying sooner

than their female counterparts. Most older men continue to enjoy the company and care of a spouse until they die—and we know that marriage is even more important to the health and happiness of men than it is to women.[43] At the same time, older men also experience less income erosion. In general, the longer retired people live, the more their income status declines—perhaps toward bare sufficiency, if not outright poverty.[44] Women are the ones who are more likely to live past seventy-five or eighty-five. The longer she lives, the more likely a married woman is to lose her spouse, and thus no longer share in the employment benefits or Social Security increments that married women get through spouses. Very old women must often struggle to get by just on Social Security and other public benefits. Likely to become disabled or chronically ill, they predominate among those who end their days in nursing homes.

Thus the portrait of Louise W in Michael Harrington's 1962 book still has considerable resonance. Yet the lonely and impoverished Louise W that Harrington discussed was seventy-three—and she may have been white, because Harrington did not say she was black. Today, Louise's fate is more likely to be that of old people in their eighties and beyond—especially women living alone, and above all isolated black women. What is more, Harrington's Louise W was more prototypical of the elderly in her day than the remaining desperately poor among all of the U.S. elderly today. This may mean that today's very poor elderly are more socially isolated and politically powerless than ever before. But there are, at least, proportionately many fewer of them than there were prior to 1962.

WHY ARE SENIORS DOING BETTER?

A prosperous national economy after World War II buoyed those destined to retire in the 1970s and beyond; yet the well-being of America's elderly at century's end is principally a story of successful accomplishments by popular and inclusive national

71

public policies. Social Security and Medicare have done an enormous amount to help older Americans—above all those in the middle and at the bottom of the economic ladder.

Riding the Postwar Economic Wave

People tend to arrive at retirement with a given accumulation of wealth and a certain potential retirement income—much of which may not be protected against erosion by inflation after they stop working. Retirees proceed to "spend down" over the course of their nonworking years. Because this pattern is so typical, it matters a lot that during the 1970s and 1980s successive cohorts of Americans retired in better and better economic shape. We have already noted this pattern for wealth holdings, particularly home ownership. Overall, "income from property made up only seven percent of the family income of the typical elderly person in 1969, but its share almost tripled to 17.2 percent by 1991."[45]

In addition, American wage and salary earners retiring in recent years have accumulated significant rights in employer-provided retirement pensions. Overall, about one-fifth of increased family income for the elderly between 1973 and 1991 comes from employment-based pensions.[46] Public employees have long enjoyed such benefits, but decent pensions in the private sector are a more recent development. Encouraged by federal tax arrangements put in place during and after World War II, employer-managed retirement pensions spread between 1950 and 1975 to cover about half of the private labor force.[47] During the 1970s, the federal government also started to regulate employer-run pension schemes, creating certain protections for employees who built up rights in those retirement systems.

But there is a catch: employment-based pensions, like accumulated wealth, mostly help people who were better-off economically prior to retirement. About half of American employees do not get pension contributions from their employers, and such retirement benefits go disproportionately to men, to unionized employees, and to those working at larger firms.[48] Employees of large firms also predominate among the small minority of employees who get retiree health benefits as a supplement to Medicare.[49] Within firms, the more an employee earns per hour, the more likely he or she is to receive private retirement benefits. Comfortably middle-class Americans, as well as upper-middle-class professionals and the truly wealthy, are thus the ones most likely to be able to supplement Social Security and Medicare with private pensions and assets, ensuring a continuation of their accustomed comfortable lifestyles during retirement.

The Huge Impact of Social Security

For all that a vibrant market economy has contributed to the well-being of those retiring in the wake of the post–World War II economic boom, the chief credit must go to public social benefits. Security for America's elderly citizens is very much an accomplishment of our democratic government. Social Security and Medicare have improved the health and economic comfort of most current retirees, allowing a phase of life that once was pleasant only for the well-to-do to be enjoyable for the majority. In 1996, the pollster and social researcher Stan Greenberg did in-depth interviews with a national selection of less-than-college-educated working Americans. With feeling, many of them told him how strongly they felt about the retirement security they hope to enjoy through Social Security and Medicare. As Greenberg summed up what he found: "retirement is a critical part of people's personal economic lives—a point of hope for stability after a lifetime of work. . . ."[50]

Viewing a comfortable old age as a reward for a lifetime of work, ordinary Americans accurately perceive their strong stake in retirement benefits. Keep in mind that elderly Americans have been less and less likely to hold jobs. In 1949, 46 percent of the earnings of elderly family heads came from employment, but by 1973 job earnings accounted for only 16 percent of total elderly family income; and by 1991 the proportion from job earnings had dropped to 9.9 percent.[51] Into the space left vacant by wages earned before retirement went increasing income from "government transfers," especially Social Security. According to economists Sheldon Danziger and Peter Gottschalk, "since World War II, rising government benefits have been the prime engine of family income growth for the elderly; by 1991 government transfers accounted for 47.5 percent of their total family income. . . ."[52] The elderly experienced an especially sizeable jump in income between 1973 and 1991, and Social Security was responsible for two-thirds of that increase.

Popularly known as "Social Security," the Old Age and Survivors Insurance (OASI) provision of the 1935 Social Security Act was steadily reworked and expanded from the 1930s to the 1970s. Surviving widows and children were added to the system's guarantees in 1939; and disabled adults were made eligible in 1956. And more and more categories of employees were folded into Social Security over the years. Particularly after eligibility was expanded in 1950 and again in 1956, the system encompassed more and more of the employed population, reaching more than 90 percent of employees by the 1960s.

In its early years, Social Security offered only modest benefits to retired workers and their dependents. "In 1950 the mean annual Social Security benefit for a retired male worker and his wife . . . amounted to about one-fifth of the median earnings of all male workers and about one-third of the poverty line for an elderly couple."[53] Subsequently, average Social Security benefits were transformed "from a retirement supplement in the 1940s and 1950s to a minimum guaranteed income by 1970 and to something well beyond the minimum by 1980."[54] By 1989, the mean benefit for a retired male worker and his wife had increased to "about two-thirds of median earnings of male workers and one and one-half times the couple's poverty line."[55]

Although Social Security by the 1960s was nearly universally inclusive of American wage earners, it still did not offer very generous retirement benefits. The breakthroughs in postwar U.S. social policy that made the biggest difference for the elderly—not just those who might have been very poor, but for middle-class people as well—clustered between the mid-1960s and the mid-1970s. Between 1968 and 1972, there were repeated hikes in average and minimum Social Security benefits; and in 1972 Social Security benefits were also indexed against erosion through inflation. Supplemental Security Income was established in 1972 to put a national minimum income floor under the most needy elderly.

Because of these major steps in national social provision, the threat of impoverishment was held at bay for most of the elderly, and middle-income Americans know that a considerable proportion of their pre-retirement income will be sustained. America's senior citizens were shielded from the vagaries of the market—at a time when market forces were about to be less kind to working-aged adults and their children. Equally important, basic pension security for the elderly has been taken completely out of the hands of the fifty states, which provide so variously (and sometimes inadequately) for the poor.

The transformations of the late 1960s and early 1970s made Social Security benefits more "redistributive"—that is, more beneficial to the modestly well-off and the least privileged wage earners—than they had been before. From the start, America's Social Security system was intended to replace only part of the wage or salary income a person made before retirement, while maintaining workers in roughly comparable status to their relative place in the income hierarchy prior to retirement. This did not change in the 1960s and 1970s; Social Security benefits are still only partial replacements for wages; and they are still set at absolutely higher levels for employees who have worked steadily at higher wages over their working lifetimes. Commentators often stress that payroll taxes for Social Security are regressive—because modest income earners pay the same rates as higher earners and there is a ceiling above which upper-middle-class and wealthy Americans no longer have to contribute portions of their salaries to Social Security. Yet changes in Social Security benefit formulas in the late 1960s and early 1970s ensured that, once they reach retirement age, people who have earned lower wages will get proportionately more generous pensions in old age than they did before these changes in benefit formulas. More privileged American employees still get absolutely larger Social Security pensions. But the "replacement rates" for modest earners and lower income earners became higher after the early 1970s reforms.

In plain English, this means that a janitor or secretary or high-school teacher now gets a Social Security pension somewhat closer to the wages he or she made at retirement, while a very highly paid manager or professional will get a Social Security pension that is not as close to what he or she made before retirement. Obviously, this helps to create a bit more comfort in retirement for regular Americans who have worked hard at low or modest pay all of their lives. And it really doesn't hurt the elite managers and professionals much, because they can combine Social Security checks with private investments and pension benefits and still do very well. Besides, the shared Social Security system has some added benefits for the more privileged beyond the sheer economic "rate of return" on payroll taxes. Should anything happen to shrink a privileged person's retirement income, he or she is assured of getting a little extra help from the shared Trust Fund. And if nothing adverse happens, that person has the satisfaction of contributing to a shared retirement system that makes America a better place for all of us together. Who wants to live in a society where hardworking janitors, secretaries, and school teachers are impoverished and demeaned in old age?

The improved "replacement rates" for low to modest earners instituted in the 1970s help to explain why Social Security has become such an effective antidote to poverty among the U.S. elderly. Without any Social Security benefits, about 50 percent of all elderly Americans would now be poor. Without the mild degree of progressivity that now exists in the payout side of the system, many more of the elderly would be below the poverty line than the 10.8 percent who now are. Although Social Security is not popularly understood as an "antipoverty policy," it is in fact America's most effective program for preventing impoverishment. Social Security spreads a modicum of comfort at the end of life to most Americans who previously worked for wages or had family ties to those who did.

Medicare and Medicaid

Another crucial set of protections for all of America's elderly came with the enactment of Medicare and Medicaid in 1965. Just about everyone sixty-five and over is enrolled in this program, which covers much of the cost of hospital and physicians' services. Before 1965, only 56 percent of Americans had hospital insurance, and if Medicare were to disappear today, more than half of the elderly would probably be uninsured or underinsured again, because health care costs have risen even faster than elderly incomes.[56]

Not that America's elderly have been relieved of the burden of health care spending. In the 1990s, older Americans continue to "spend an average of 14 percent of their after-tax incomes on health care, compared to 4 percent for the rest of the population."[57] Not surprisingly, the financial burdens get heavier as advancing age leads to the need for more treatment or help. Seniors must pay premiums for Medicare coverage, and all except the poorest must cover "deductibles" for hospital stays. In addition, many of the elderly pay a lot for items not covered by Medicare, including prescription drugs and special kinds of at-home or long-term care. The average share of elderly income spent on health care today is actually more than seniors spent before Medicare and Medicaid were created.[58] Of course, elderly family incomes were smaller in those earlier times, before enhancements in Social Security, so the proportions spent then on health care represented a bigger burden.

Despite continuing health expenses for the elderly, Medicare and Medicaid have made a huge difference. They have given older men and women full access to the services of doctors and hospitals, while buffering them against the rapid inflation of medical costs of the 1970s and 1980s. Over three-quarters of Medicare beneficiaries have incomes below $25,000 a year, and the average spending for each Medicare recipient is about one-fifth of that. If people had to pay cash for the equivalent of Medicare benefits plus the additional care they now pay for out-of-pocket, such a burden would devastate the standard of living of many elderly households each year and counteract the overall growth in elderly income that has been achieved through Social Security. Millions of older men and (especially) women would simply do without medical care. Our grandfathers and grandmothers would need much more help from their children and grandchildren. Or else they would die sooner, and live in greater discomfort than they now do.

Although Medicaid is ostensibly targeted mainly at poor mothers and children, it also helps nearly 4 million elderly Americans. Medicaid shelters many (although not all) of the very poorest seniors from what might otherwise be unaffordable out-of-pocket costs associated with Medicare. Even middle-class families, after they have depleted their assets to a certain point, benefit from the more than two-thirds of Medicaid spending that goes for long-term nursing-home care for disabled elderly persons.[59] Only about 5 percent of the elderly, mostly very old women, are in nursing homes, yet for these extremely fragile people, Medicaid is a vital lifeline. "Two-thirds of Americans in nursing homes receive assistance from Medicaid, which pays for a little less than half of the nation's entire nursing home bill."[60]

From the point of view of helping the elderly, a problem with Medicaid has been that many elderly people who might be eligible for its benefits do not apply for them. Many Americans—including the elderly—find it demeaning to apply to a "welfare" program that requires proof of low income and assets before eligibility is established. Clearly, American retired people of modest as well as better economic means appreciate the universality of Medicare and Social Security, the absence of embarrassing "means tests" and the sense that benefits in these programs go by right to all former employees and their dependents.

Universally available public programs have encouraged full access and improved health care for old people. The result has been longer life and greater contentment. U.S. life expectancy "plateaued" between 1954 and 1968, and then improved in the 1970s and 1980s. "It is probably not coincidental," point out Treas and Torrecilha, "that the increases in life expectancy followed the 1966 implementation of Medicare. Older Americans' greater use of preventive health care services, for example, led to widespread detection and treatment of high blood pressure, a condition increasing the risk of cardiovascular disease."[61]

Older Americans are happy with their health care situation, too, an important matter in its own right. "In 1993, 94 percent of Medicare beneficiaries said they were satisfied with the ease of getting a physician visit, 94 percent had great confidence in their doctor, and 97 percent said they had no trouble getting care during the past year."[62] These are outstanding indications of satisfaction in a nation where many working-aged Americans and their children still do not have any basic health insurance at all, and where workers who do have coverage through employment are experiencing ever-greater restrictions on their choice of doctors and hospitals. Thirty years of Medicare and Medicaid have created a relatively commodious health care situation for elderly Americans—compared to the situation older Americans experienced before 1965, and also compared to the situation faced by many Americans under sixty-five today.

THE ELDERLY IN AMERICAN POLITICS

If public programs have made such a big difference for older Americans, how did this come about? For many observers the answer seems obvious: The elderly have used disproportionate political clout—"Gray Power"—to get more for themselves through government, while other more worthy but less politically powerful groups have been shortchanged. In the evocative picture painted by the Concord Coalition's Peter Peterson:

> I once asked artist Saul Steinberg how he might paint his vision of America as seen from Washington—a parallel to his famous picture of a New Yorker's vision of the world. In the foreground of the picture, we would see as giants the organizations aimed at protecting entitlements for today's retired and elderly Americans: the AARP (American Association of Retired Persons), SOS (Save Our Security), the NCSC (National Council of Senior Citizens), and the Gray Panthers, plus another thirty-five-odd pressure groups that claim a combined membership of 100 million. . . .
>
> And what about the backdrop of Steinberg's picture? There, diminutive in size, we would find the young working families who foot the bills for our public entitlements. Along with them, but only as tiny specks of dust on the map of our approach to governing America, we might also catch a glimpse of America's children and grandchildren. . . .[63]

Offering a slightly different twist on the same argument, Harvard political scientist Paul E. Peterson (no relation to Peter Peterson) offers "An Immodest Proposal: Let's Give Children the Vote." He contrasts public spending on children versus the elderly, and attributes the big tilt in favor of the old to "the voting power of the elderly, the clout exercised by" the AARP, and "the increasing size of the elderly population." "But in 1990," Peterson points out,

> there were twice as many children under the age of 18 (65 million) as senior citizens (32 million). If children were enfranchised, fundamental policy changes would certainly follow. Groups representing children would immediately acquire status and power, they would frighten politicians with organized letter-writing cam-

paigns, . . . [and] they would demand a bigger share of the welfare pie. . . .[64]

Both of these Petersons—Peter and Paul—offer a model of U.S. democracy and public policy making in which social programs and the generational distribution of public spending are a simple function of age-based voting power and interest-group "clout." But the two Petersons do not fully understand American politics. Their polemics offer a very partial and skewed picture of why social protections for the elderly have flourished in American democracy.

Was It Really Gray Power?

There are, to be sure, facts that can be marshaled in support of the Gray Power thesis. Elderly Americans represented only 8 percent of the population in 1950, but now they are 12.5 percent, or one in eight Americans; and the proportion of elderly in the population is headed upward. The American Association of Retired Persons *is* the "eight hundred pound gorilla" of U.S. associations by any measure—with a membership totaling more than half of Americans aged fifty and over, its paid staff of 1,700 (1,200 of them in Washington), its budget of about $500 million a year, its nationwide network of subsidized volunteer activists, and its remarkable network of services and publications, including the country's largest-circulation magazine, *Modern Maturity*.[65]

What is more, since 1980 older Americans (especially the younger elderly) have voted considerably more often than younger American adults. As political scientist Andrea Campbell explains, in "the presidential elections of the 1950s, 1960s and 1970s, seniors voted at the same or lower rates than nonseniors," but "beginning in 1980 a shift occurred as senior participation outstripped that of nonseniors. Overall, senior voting participation in presidential election years has risen from 73 percent in 1952 to 83 percent in 1996."[66] In contrast, nonsenior turnout peaked at 79 percent in 1960, then declined to 68 percent in 1988, before rebounding a bit to 74 percent in 1992 and 1996. The contrast between elderly and nonelderly voting is even greater in midterm (non-presidential) elections. And seniors are also more likely to contribute money and volunteer time to political campaigns.

There is little question that elderly advocates outweigh and outmaneuver advocates for children in both state and national politics. With seniors accounting for a fifth or more of votes in elections, U.S. politicians regard older voters and their advocacy organizations as influential forces. When political scientists Fay Lomax Cook and Edith Barrett asked Congressional representatives "from whom they hear the most among their constituents" on social-welfare issues, they found that "an overwhelming number of Congress members mention the elderly and groups representing the elderly."[67] One representative estimated that of about 200 people who came each month to public meetings he held for constituents, some 150 would be elderly citizens worried about Social Security. Another representative explained to Cook and Barrett that the "seniors are much in the forefront because of their . . . capabilities of contacting individually and through organizations. They have very active organizations—effective organizations. I think that they do represent a very large constituency in voting percentile."[68]

The concerns of older people certainly can influence public opinion and sway legislative outcomes. During the 1993–94 battle over President Bill Clinton's Health Security plan, for example, elderly Americans became worried in the fall of 1993 about what Clinton's proposals might mean for Medicare. Never adequately addressed, the worries of seniors became harbingers of an overall shift in public opinion against comprehensive health reforms.[69] A similar process unfolded again during 1995 and 1996, when conservative Republicans proposed huge cuts in Medicare spending in the context of their so-called revolution, which aimed simultaneously to cut taxes and eliminate the federal budget deficit. Again, worries about Medicare soon surfaced, and public opinion shifted against the Republicans, who not only lost the 1996 presidential contest but came close to losing control of the Congress as well.[70]

Many facts thus confirm that older Americans are a political force. But other facts raise real doubts about the red-meat version of the Gray Power thesis—the proposition that the elderly are a selfish and overweening "special interest group." On most public policy questions, it turns out, elderly Americans are far from an attitudinal monolith. They usually do not think very differently from younger adults. And the political viability of programs for the elderly depends on more generalized support than the elderly alone provide.

Only around a third of older Americans report a strong identification with "the elderly" as a category, because most continue to think in terms of the partisan and group identifications to which they have previously been attached.[71] Different subgroups of the elderly vary in their support for "spending more" on programs for seniors, with poorer retirees—the ones who depend the most on Social Security—joining liberals in support of spending more, while better-off seniors and conservatives are more inclined to favor maintaining spending on the elderly at current levels.

As we have seen, elderly Americans have become more active in electoral politics than other Americans. Notice, however, that this divergence came in the 1980s, *after* generous social spending for retirees was already in place. Rather than "Gray Power" leading to new government programs, America's elder security programs have themselves helped to encourage and facilitate higher levels of civic engagement by seniors at all income levels. In turn, such across-the-board engagement by the elderly alerts politicians to their concerns and helps to sustain Social Security, Medicare, and other public programs on which so many retirees depend.[72] Even here, the case should not be overstated. Vast majorities of ordinary Americans of all ages want Social Security and Medicare to be either preserved or made more generous, so there is not much "variance" to be explained. Yet what variance there is takes a surprising direction: American adults between thirty-one and fifty-nine are a bit more likely to support public generosity toward the elderly than are the oldsters themselves.[73]

Most Americans do not think public supports for the elderly hurt younger citizens. Quite the contrary! Despite the constant drumbeat of propaganda about "generational warfare" and "old versus young" coming from advocacy groups, media pundits, and certain social science experts, most Americans simply do not see matters in such terms. "Generational conflict" is a statistical accounting device appealing to social scientists—as well as a catchy slogan useful for dramatizing yet another national "crisis"— but this notion is out of touch with how people actually live.

Large numbers of adult Americans are in close contact with their elderly parents, and thus are likely to share values and information with them. Although adult generations in America rarely live in the same households, many of them do live close by in the same communities, and others converse regularly by telephone or in letters.[74] Some 59 percent of adults report being in touch with their mothers at least once a week; and 20 percent claim to have daily contact.[75] "From one fourth to one third of adult children," moreover, "help their mothers or fathers and receive help from them on everyday kinds of tasks such as running errands and babysitting."[76] Adult daughters are the ones closest in touch, especially with their own mothers.

For families, the comfort and independence of grandmother and grandfather is a very good thing. Most people love their elderly relatives. And if the old folks are comfortable in old age, that makes aging easier for their offspring to contemplate. Besides, if grandparents have enough economic security and good health to continue to live in independent households, life becomes easier for their children and grandchildren. The generations may still converse and visit, but at least they are not on top of one another day to day. Adults in midlife know they are fortunate not to have to worry much about paying—current or anticipated—bills for grandma's or grandpa's medical care or regular living expenses. That frees up the earnings of working-aged adults to pay for other things, including the care and education of their own children.

In the final analysis, if grandma and grandpa are relatively secure, they can make vital contributions to others. They can volunteer in the community—and we know that older Americans are, in fact, the most frequent group participants and volunteers in our society.[77] Within individual families, elders can babysit for their grandchildren, thus helping their adult children. They can contribute toward a home mortgage or a college education. And they can make bequests of accumulated assets. Research on intergenerational transfers that takes into account such private flows, as well as the flows of taxes and expenditures through government, documents that very major contributions of time and money are made by elders to help their adult children and their grandchildren. As policy analysts Karl Kronebusch and Mark Schlesinger sum up, "we estimate that . . . intergenerational private transfers account for $1.1 trillion, . . . more than double the magnitude of government cash transfer programs." They note that the "bulk of private transfers flows down the age spectrum— from parents to their children. Most Americans are net recipients with respect to their parents, and all, except the oldest old, are net givers to their children. . . . Elders as a group give more than they receive in the sphere of private transfers. They are net dependents only in the public sphere of government transfers and benefits."[78]

The well-being of old and young are tied together in all these ways and for all these reasons—as ordinary Americans understand. Women, especially, perceive and value generational interdependence. The elite language of "generational conflict" may resonate among a small minority of very privileged and upwardly mobile yuppies, especially men. They are the ones least likely to be closely in touch with their own parents. But Americans who are *not* highly paid, jet-setting professionals or managers are very likely to be in close touch with their parents. And ordinary Americans would be badly hurt if grandparents became less secure and retirement became unappealing. Thus it is not so surprising that most Americans support—and very much want to sustain—Medicare and Social Security. People sense, quite accurately, that these supreme achievements of American democracy are capstones of the good life for most Americans.

Elder Organizations and Public Policy Making

The notion that Gray Power explains the nation's generosity toward the elderly becomes even more questionable once we look at how things actually unfolded. As we have already seen, policy breakthroughs toward something approximating social generosity for the elderly occurred between the mid-1960s and the mid-1970s. But the big bursts of formation of advocacy groups for the elderly did not occur until the 1970s and afterwards.[79]

True enough, some key players in today's elderly advocacy group system came into existence in the late 1950s and early 1960s. The National Council of Senior Citizens (NCSC) was formed in 1961 and the much touted AARP was launched in 1958. Only the NCSC was oriented to national politics and social policy making from its inception, however. The AARP was little involved in campaigning for national legislation until *after* the policy breakthroughs of the 1960s and early 1970s.

The NCSC could be seen as an agent of "Gray Power"—or at least gray initiative—because as it was launched during the early 1960s, this group played an active role in agitating for the enactment of Medicare in 1965.[80] The NCSC was also very active in pressing Congress for the improvements in average and minimum Social Security benefits that were legislated between 1968 and 1972.[81] But two caveats are very much in order. For one thing, scholars who have investigated the expansion of Social Security and the enactment of Medicare assign the NCSC at most a minor, supporting role. According to political scientist

Martha Derthick, the key players behind the Social Security expansions were officials of the Social Security Administration, who had long been planning such changes, and key Congressional representatives, especially Chairman Wilbur Mills of the House Ways and Means Committee.[82] The same actors turn up as well in the rendition of the founding of Medicare by political scientist Theodore Marmor.[83] And public opinion analyst Lawrence Jacobs argues convincingly that broad public support—from Americans of all ages—played a role in the founding of Medicare. In 1964 and 1965, this proposed new program was seen as appealingly modeled on a universal, non–means-tested, social insurance program with which people were already happily familiar: namely Social Security itself.[84]

Another problem with any suggestion that Gray Power lay behind the 1960s–early 1970s breakthroughs in social provision for the elderly has to do with the big role the organized labor movement and the Democratic Party played in launching the NCSC in the first place.[85] The nascent NCSC was "sponsored" by the AFL-CIO trade union movement, whose retiree clubs were among its local seedbeds. The NCSC was also encouraged by— and partly rooted in networks left over from—the "Senior Citizens for Kennedy" effort stimulated by the Democrats during the 1960 campaign to elect John F. Kennedy to the presidency. The NCSC was originally, and remains to the present, part of the "labor-liberal" complex in U.S. national politics, a set of alliances and resources that was very substantial back in the 1960s, but very much on the wane today. This is not to say that the NCSC is not a "genuine" old people's movement. It is. But its goals, resources, and clout are part of a broader movement.

The AARP, the chief elder advocacy organization outside the labor movement, was virtually irrelevant to the public policy breakthroughs of the 1960s and early 1970s. Founded in 1958 through the collaboration of a retired teacher and principal with a young insurance entrepreneur, the AARP initially offered group life insurance and market-based services to a predominately middle-class membership.[86] In the early years, the AARP did not even have its headquarters in Washington, D.C., and its public affairs staff was miniscule. Working cooperatively with the American Medical Association, the AARP originally sponsored health legislation very different from the universal social insurance of Medicare that was eventually enacted in 1965.[87] When the AARP became more involved in politics during the late 1960s and the 1970s, its chief priority was getting rid of legally mandated retirement, a goal appealing to the middle-class elderly.[88] The AARP did *not* push for the Social Security changes of 1968–73—although it did not oppose them, either.

After Medicare was enacted and the middle-class elderly were more fully incorporated into a more generous Social Security system, the AARP became much more engaged in advocacy for these programs. Given the actual sequence of events, it would make much more sense to say that transformations in U.S. security programs for the elderly impacted upon the strength and orientation of the AARP than it would to say that the AARP brought about these federal policy changes in the first place. (Interestingly enough, the same sequence happened back in the nineteenth century: The initial expansions of Civil War benefits occurred when the Grand Army of the Republic [GAR] was in organizational disarray and not much involved in legislative lobbying; but after federal benefits became significant, the GAR expanded its membership and became much more involved in public policy struggles.)

By the 1980s, the AARP—along with the NCSC and dozens of other, more specialized elderly advocacy groups—had become a significant player in the interest-group politics of Washington. A 1982 *National Journal* "political report" on this lobbying system was tellingly entitled "The Elderly as a Political Force—26 Million Strong and Well Organized."[89] During the 1980s, the AARP and most other elderly advocacy groups moved into a close working relationship with Congressional Democrats, seeking to protect programs for the elderly during the Reagan era of tax cuts and criticism of "big government." Of course, it was also during the 1980s that pundits began to portray the AARP as an all-powerful juggernaut.

But even now that the AARP has become huge, and devotes a significant fraction of its resources to monitoring public policy and lobbying Congress and the executive branch, caution about its political clout remains in order. Two examples—the enactment and sudden repeal of the Medicare Catastrophic Coverage Act of 1988, and the Health Security episode under President Bill Clinton in 1993–94—underline the limits of AARP power in social policy making.

In the Catastrophic Coverage drama, the AARP urged Congress to enact a bill to protect elderly patients against open-ended hospital costs and unusually high expenditures on prescription drugs. With Republican president Reagan's support, Congress enacted this first significant expansion of Medicare coverage since 1965.[90] But Congress was legislating in an era of budget constraints, so it required that well-to-do elderly subscribers to Medicare pay a new surtax to cover all of the cost of these new "catastrophic" benefits. Urged on by small advocacy organizations competing with the AARP, wealthier seniors unleashed a fierce mobilization against the Catastrophic Act, pushing for its repeal even after it was signed into law. Privileged seniors hated the unprecedented special "seniors' tax," and they did not feel they would benefit from the new Catastrophic Coverage legislation. The AARP staff in Washington continued to support the Catastrophic Act, believing that they stood for the interests of most senior citizens. But the AARP leadership was badly burned in this episode. In the end, Congress repealed the law. The competing advocacy group that led the charge against Catastrophic Coverage, the National Council to Protect Social Security and Medicare, gained resources and leverage because of discontent with the AARP on the part of some seniors.

Five years later, the national leadership of the AARP again became interested in an extension of health coverage—this time, in the Health Security plan fashioned during 1993 by the fledgling Democratic administration of President Bill Clinton. Administration planners worked closely with AARP leaders, incorporating into the Health Security proposal significant new benefits for millions of elderly citizens. Health Security was to include a new prescription drug benefit, and also the beginnings of coverage for long-term care during chronic illnesses at the end of life. AARP leaders liked these benefits and supported universal health coverage for Americans of all ages. But they were worried about repeating the Catastrophic Coverage episode, by "getting out in front" of their millions of members. Polls showed that many seniors were worried that the Clinton administration would use big cuts in Medicare to pay for Health Security. In the end, the AARP leadership temporized, and did not get strongly behind the Clinton administration's efforts.[91] Ironically, the AARP's reluctance to take an out-front role in the battle for Health Security probably helped to undermine a comprehensive reform of the nation's generationally skewed system of health care financing—a reform that, had it passed, would have helped to protect against a deepening conservative turn against governmental generosity to the elderly.[92]

The AARP, it turns out, is not so much the Gray Power tyrannosaur as it is the lumbering brontosaurus of contemporary U.S. politics. Built around a set of market-oriented discount services for America's citizens aged fifty and above, the AARP is now so large and internally diverse that it cannot move with force and alacrity in policy battles. Its members may often disagree on key policy issues. And its liberal-leaning staff leadership and self-appointed activists can find themselves at odds with underlying mass elderly sentiments—especially those of the more well-to-do seniors who are most articulate and involved in national politics.

As any big, wealthy bureaucracy tends to be, the AARP is cautious. It has a lot of economic stakes that could be compromised—or enhanced—depending on shifting policy outcomes and partisan climates. Looking back, many of the seemingly "liberal" stances of the AARP seem to have depended on Democratic control of Congress during the 1980s and early 1990s. Now that conservative Republicans are a force in Washington and influential in national electoral politics, the AARP has become more cagey than ever. During 1998, certain AARP leaders even flirted with schemes for partially privatizing Social Security. While such flirtation proved short-lived, the AARP will probably continue to be more effective in defending previous security gains for the elderly than in fighting for any new ones.

The Big Picture

If Gray Power does not explain the breakthroughs in Social Security and Medicare of the 1960s and 1970s, what does? Stepping back and taking a broader look—reminding ourselves of what we learned in Chapter Two about U.S. social provision since the Civil War—we can see that American democracy has repeatedly been relatively generous to the elderly. But the creation and expansion of public social benefits for the elderly have never been primarily the achievements of the elderly themselves. Instead, a combination of other conditions has pertained each time the nation has acted to help many, or all, of our grandparents.

A widespread cultural sense that older Americans are "deserving" of public support has been important each time government benefits have been expanded. So have partisan and group allies acting in national politics. And so have key national governmental capacities, both administrative and fiscal. These conditions came together in the late nineteenth century, when benefits for Union veterans and survivors of the Civil War evolved into an extraordinarily generous system of disability, survivors, and old-age pensions, as well as old-age homes, for a large fraction of America's elderly men, particularly in the North. These benefits originally expanded before most Union veterans reached their sixties; and generous Civil War benefits depended for support on public attitudes and political alliances that went well beyond the veterans themselves and their organizations. Elderly protection through Civil War benefits also depended on a federal treasury swollen with tariff revenues, which in turn were championed by a strong Republican Party.

Exactly the same sorts of points can be made about Social Security and its later programmatic additions, including Medicare. Once again, Social Security's old-age insurance provisions were launched long before they came to benefit large numbers of the elderly. The programs had—and still have—strong cross-generational support. And these remarkably politically successful social insurance programs depended for their "maturation" on favorable administrative and fiscal conditions. They grew up while America's federal government was well financed and not deeply in debt; and they expanded while working-aged taxpayers were both demographically numerous and taking home rising wages in a buoyant postwar economy. Social Security and Medicare, in short, were not impositions by sinister Gray Powerites. They were broad democratic achievements propelled by American voters and taxpayers of all ages.

WHAT DOES THE FUTURE HOLD?

Michael Harrington would be delighted by most of the changes for America's elderly that have occurred since he published *The Other America*. Especially between the mid-1960s and the mid-1970s, the citizens of the United States made a real commitment to build on the foundations laid in the 1935 Social Security Act, fashioning comprehensive and generous protections for the health and economic security of senior citizens. Additional problems still need to be addressed, including the extreme poverty of some very old women, and the challenge of financing and providing long-term care for seniors who are not acutely ill but still need assistance in their homes and communities. Still, most of America's elderly at century's end live out their years with considerable security and a sense that they are socially honored and protected after lifetimes of work and care for others.

We Americans can be proud of the achievements of our late-twentieth-century war against privation among the elderly—yet we should also worry about the future of our past policy achievements. Despite all that broad-based Social Security and Medicare have done to make retirement a pleasant stage of life for Americans of modest means while putting a floor under the very poor, these programs are now the target of quite extreme proposals for radical restructuring. The problem is not some huge upsurge of popular resentment of the elderly. Most Americans neither perceive nor want generational warfare in social policy. But grave challenges are nevertheless upon us. Pundits and politicians are debating the reconstruction of our social policies, with Social Security, Medicare, and the future of national social provision for the elderly at the vortex of those debates.

Certain dilemmas are inescapably grounded in changing demographic realities for which we should, on the whole, be grateful. Growing old may be worrisome but (as the popular joke asks) what is the alternative? Happily, Americans are living longer—and retirement is seen as a positive stage of life, when new interests and commitments can be pursued. Perhaps what's good for individuals is not so good for society, though. The huge "baby boom" generation that was born after World War II is now headed toward retirement. When boomers begin to retire in large numbers from 2010 onward, joining even older Americans who live into their eighties and nineties, the U.S. population will be fundamentally reconfigured. There will be many fewer working adults in relation to retirees; and projected public spending for existing kinds of pensions and elder services is scheduled to skyrocket.

Scary scenarios can be envisaged on the basis of the demographic realities I have just mentioned—such as the notion that working Americans will have to pay up to 80 percent of their incomes in taxes to carry the load of costly benefits for their elders.[93] These scenarios are not believable. U.S. social benefits have never remained exactly the same over such long stretches of time; and long-term projections are subject to so many tricky manipulations that—no surprise!—they always turn out predicting just what the given propagandist wants to project.[94]

Today's doomsayers fail to note that as the proportion of elderly people in the U.S. population grows, the proportion of children needing economic and parental investments will decline.[95] The overall ratio of "dependent" children and elderly in relation to working-aged Americans will not change much; and there will in fact be more working adults in relation to children and retirees in 2030 than there were in 1965.[96] And we're not just talking about fewer little kids, either. As pointed out in colorful speeches by Bruce Vladeck (formerly of the Department of Health and Human Services), an aging society means fewer teenagers. That alone is bound to save society a lot of money— and worry.

Too much can be made of the proportions of people projected for various age categories. Our nation's ability to care for young and old depends not just on numbers of people but on how well the economy does. Many projections of future demographic doom and unbearable tax burdens for Social Security and Medicare are based on suspiciously low projections of national economic growth (and these doomsday projections are often made by the same pundits who simultaneously presume that Wall Street investments will grow at an amazing pace!). However, if we find ways to keep our national economy growing, and if we make wise choices about taxes and investments for the future, we will easily be able to handle the costs of caring for our children and grandchildren in the twenty-first century.[97] As people in the United States have learned since 1992, many problems are solved, or at least mitigated, in a growing national economy. Just a few years ago, fiscal conservatives claimed that the United States would be destroyed by the federal budget deficit; but a decade of robust economic growth generated the additional tax revenues to erase that deficit.

For the longer run, much depends on how well-educated,

healthy, and productive the working adults of the future turn out to be—just as much depends on the quality of the private capital and public arrangements through which their efforts will be channeled. Proportionately more working-aged adults can certainly provide for themselves, their children, and their retired or partially retired parents—*if* the U.S. economy of the twenty-first century has well-trained, highly motivated employees using state-of-the-art equipment. In any event, many of the productive activities of the next century will focus on health care and education—and, indeed, on services for the elderly. So these are not just "costs" for the country to pay. They are activities at which working and taxpaying Americans will be able to build careers and make their livings, while helping others.

When we come right down to it, the biggest "crises" that Social Security and Medicare face today are political rather than demographic. There are population shifts to be faced, certainly, but we Americans are approaching these shifts with "crisis" rhetoric because a sense of impending demographic disaster has been stoked for essentially political reasons.[98] As we saw in Chapter Two, conservatives opposed to the size and scope of federal government activities have taken advantage of population aging in the context of generational imbalances in post-1960s U.S. social provision. Campaigning to break up social programs that include middle-class as well as less-privileged American retirees, conservatives invoke the coming demographic transitions of the twenty-first century to argue that Social Security and Medicare are no longer viable. They hope that Americans will look at selected projections and be stampeded into slashing shared public programs for the elderly in the name of helping "our children and grandchildren" win some abstract generational war.

When it comes to specific "reforms," conservatives aim to substitute individualized and market-oriented health and pension programs for the shared and tax-financed features of Medicare and Social Security. For example, both Republicans and conservative Democrats on the National Bipartisan Commission on the

Future of Medicare (set up by Congress as part of the 1997 federal budget agreement) proposed to abandon universal guarantees of specified health coverage for the elderly. To resolve a
supposed "crisis" in Medicare, many of the commissioners would
allow private insurance companies and managed care plans to
compete on artificially favorable terms with the public system.
Each senior would get a fixed amount of money, a kind of
voucher, and be told to buy the insurance plan of his or her
choice. "Supporters of this approach say . . . that it could save
money because [elderly] beneficiaries would be more sensitive to
prices and premiums, and would shop around for the best deal."[99]
This claim is "without definitive proof," explains *New York Times*
reporter Robert Pear, because data to date do not show that private managed care plans necessarily save much money, especially
not on sick or elderly patients. Pear also notes the concern of
critics within and beyond the Medicare commission that, with
fixed vouchers, "elderly beneficiaries would be more exposed to
financial risks and ruin if health costs rose more than expected, as
has often happened."

Under the reforms proposed by conservatives, elderly Americans would end up fragmented into many different insurance
groupings, as private plans endeavor to enroll the wealthiest and
the healthiest and leave the sick and the poor to be covered by
shrinking public resources. While the most privileged Americans
could supplement Medicare vouchers with their own or employer
resources to buy high-quality care, many other Americans would
be relegated to a dwindling Medicare system overwhelmed by sick
and needy patients. Americans of modest means who opted to
join private managed care plans might often find themselves
unable to afford needed care within the fixed allocation. To buy
good care, they would have to contribute on their own.

"At stake in the . . . Medicare debate," writes citizen activist Kip
Sullivan, "is not just the fairness and sufficiency of Medicare
funding, but whether health care for America's elderly will be
turned over to the insurance industry which has made such a

mess of health care for the non-elderly."[100] If Medicare is broken up, seniors will be subjected to the same adverse trends as everyone else: receding coverage, rising co-payments, and hassles with managed care bureaucracies trying to cut costs. Hardly a progressive move. And a politically fraught change as well. For in a partially privatized Medicare system, seniors would be much less able to band together politically to correct shortfalls. As conservatives understand full well, broadly shared public social programs encourage cross-class political alliances to defend and extend social provision, while individualized, market-oriented programs make it easier to further limit or slash taxes and public spending.

For Social Security, meanwhile, a variety of overhaul plans were put onto the public agenda by the 1994–96 Social Security Advisory Council.[101] All thirteen members of this commission agreed that Social Security's taxes and benefits may need adjustment in the next century to meet the challenge of baby boom retirements. But commissioners divided into three camps about possible directions for reform, dramatizing the contrast between shared adjustments in Social Security and the plans conservatives espouse to break it into individual investment accounts—either all at once, or step by step.

Arguing along lines advocated in purer market forms by conservative economists Milton Friedman and Martin Feldstein, one group of five on the 1994–96 Advisory Council argued for the individualization of retirement savings.[102] Under their "Personal Security Account" plan, the nation would over time divert most payroll taxes and shared Social Security funds into regulated individual investment accounts. All workers would be guaranteed a sub-poverty-level flat pension, but otherwise what each person gets during retirement would depend on how well the economy grew and on how adroitly he or she arranged to invest mandated "contributions" through Wall Street.

Under this plan, each American employee would still have to pay the equivalent of today's payroll taxes—or more—but how much he or she got after retirement would be due to his or her own astuteness and luck. Results would follow lines of education and class background on average, since the more privileged would be more experienced investors and would have more money to manipulate. Above the minimal floor, each person would be on her or his own, and vast inequities could result, even among those who started at similar levels. Some retirees might end up in abject poverty, while other retirees might do very well. And if the national economy and Wall Street took sharp downturns just as some groups were retiring, well, too bad. Younger Americans would not have to help the unlucky retirees in those circumstances, because there would be only minimal national promises to be kept.

Another group of six Advisory Council members, led by Robert Ball, the former Social Security Commissioner who wants to preserve our shared system, pointed out that Wall Street profits can easily be harnessed for Social Security without breaking the system into millions of individual accounts—or paying broker fees for those accounts! The Ball "Maintenance of Benefits" plan would slightly adjust payroll taxes and the age at which retirees become eligible to collect full benefits. Otherwise, though, the Ball plan would simply allow Social Security trustees, acting as public investment managers, to channel part of the Social Security Trust Fund for investments in market securities. A higher rate of return might well be obtained, and such profits would then flow into the shared Social Security fund. The nation as a whole would continue to guarantee pretty much the present kind and level of benefits to future retirees. A version of this idea for shared market investment of part of Social Security's funds was subsequently endorsed by President Clinton in his 1999 State of the Union address. This approach lets Social Security tap the benefits of national economic growth and a rising stock market, without the costly broker fees or increased personal risk that individual market-accounts would entail.

Finally, the smallest faction of 1994–96 Advisory Council

members, a team of two led by chairman Ned Gramlich, offered a supposedly middle-of-the-road option—exactly the sort of complicated "compromise" that new Democrats at the Democratic Leadership Coucil (DLC) tend to espouse these days. The Gramlich plan is actually a combined tax increase and partial individualization of Social Security. It calls for raising existing payroll taxes, but diverting the increment into publicly regulated but market-based personal investment accounts. Americans would eventually collect pensions in part from the shared Social Security system, and in part from their individual accounts (whose appreciation would be influenced by luck and smart investment choices).

This approach is the privatization camel's nose under the tent. It builds on the familiarity that many Americans, especially the privileged, already have with tax-subsidized "401K" savings-investment accounts, and aims to give more people a stake in such market investments. Although additional risk is bound to accompany this, Gramlich claims his plan would not be as radical a step as full individual-privatization, because most of people's Social Security pensions would still come from the system of shared taxes and benefits. On the conservative end of the Democratic Party, the DLC has endorsed ideas along the lines of the Gramlich scheme.[103] And many on Wall Street would be delighted at this "incremental" approach, for it would channel new business to private investment managers and serve as an entering wedge for shifting more and more of the nation's savings toward Wall Street.[104]

Indeed, for all that it is so touted by powerful elites, the Gramlich approach is not truly a "compromise." It would start the ball rolling toward more and more upper-middle-class withdrawal from the shared—and redistributive—Social Security system that has done so much to sustain middle-income as well as low-income earners in retirement. If individual accounts were built directly into "Social Security" as a second tier, many Americans—and especially the most privileged who want to manipulate their own savings—would soon press to divert payroll taxes into the individual accounts. During periods of market upturn, people could imagine that improvements in their pensions accrued mostly from the individual-accounts portion of the revised Social Security system. Barred from investing in market securities, the shared and redistributive portion of Social Security would lose ground and look less and less attractive. Facing tax resistance, after ten to fifteen years shared Social Security could easily dwindle into a residual welfare program. Thus, the goals of the privatizers would be achieved through the back door.

In the end "partial privatization" schemes should be opposed by progressives just as fiercely as complete individualization plans. Like a total breakup of social insurance into "personal" accounts, partial privatization would in due course eviscerate, rather than refurbish, Social Security as Americans know it.

Privatizing Medicare and Social Security would surely lead to more inequality and insecurity. Indeed, restructuring might well end up undoing the progress against elderly privation that occurred after the 1960s. If Medicare is broken up into a series of subsidies for private managed care plans, and if Social Security is even partially diverted into individual accounts on Wall Street, gaps will widen between the privileged and Americans of middling and lower incomes. Millions of the very old, especially women, will fall between widening cracks in a market-dominated health care system. If privatizing schemes succeed, most Americans may, before long, look back longingly at an all-too-brief "golden era" for retirees—the interval after Social Security and Medicare were fully established and before they were set on the road to "privatization."

Can Americans, instead, readjust shared social insurance programs to ride through the coming demographic transition to a "grayer" society? In principle, the answer is certainly yes. As I will discuss more fully in Chapter Five, there are very good ways to readjust Social Security and Medicare that are socially shared, preserving them as honorable and adequate protections for all of

America's current and future grandparents. But whether the available options to proceed in shared ways are actually taken depends, not on inexorable demographic givens, but on social alliances, moral vision, and wise political choices.

Before further engaging the debate about the future of social protections for America's grandparents, let us examine what is happening to children and working-aged parents. The fates of generational groups are fully intertwined, both politically and economically. In the face of conservative counterattacks, the future of social supports for the elderly depends on the political will of the majority of Americans—just as public funding for retiree protections depends on a healthy economy buoyed by the efforts of today's and tomorrow's working adults. To make wise reconstructions of U.S. social policies possible, we need to think of all age groups together, considering what it will take to ensure opportunity and security for all Americans—across classes and generations alike.

CHAPTER FOUR

Our Children and Their Overstretched Parents

AMERICA IS AWASH in talk about children and families. Throughout the 1990s, the drumbeat has gone on. In 1991, a bipartisan National Commission on Children issued its final report, calling for "all Americans to work together to change the conditions that jeopardize the health and well-being of so many of our youngest citizens and threaten our future as an economic power, a democratic nation, and a caring society."[1] Years later, most of the recommendations of the National Commission remain unfulfilled, although everyone seems to be talking about America's children.

Foundations sponsor task forces and reports.[2] Leading authors publish stirring manifestos.[3] And commercial advertisements tout business-sponsored projects to help kids and families. Open any airline magazine these days, or walk into any Wal-Mart super-store, and you are likely to see proclamations of the ways managers or employees are "volunteering" to help children. There will be no mention of things the business or the store may have done to reduce taxes or benefits, throw employees out of work, cut wages for young workers, or undercut community institutions. No matter what they are actually doing in practice, businesses have learned the public relations value of proclaiming support for families and communities.

Politicians talk a good game, too. Congressional Democrats

have rallied behind a "Families First" agenda, and Republicans proclaim their desire to "save children" from destructive welfare programs and to help "the American family" with big tax cuts.[4] During the 1996 presidential-election season, the Republican convention featured as its keynote speaker Representative Susan Molinari holding her three-month-old infant daughter, while the Democratic convention in Chicago played up parental issues and highlighted President Clinton's (then) sixteen-year-old daughter, Chelsea. Both of America's major political parties want to be perceived as supportive of families, parents, and children. But in U.S. politics these days, talk and television images can readily mask inaction—or even movement in the opposite direction from the values ostensibly proclaimed.

If bitterly divided politicians and pundits argue more than they act to help families and children, that is partly because America is in a period of partisan and intellectual polarization—especially when it comes to family matters. Despite the pro-children cacophony, there is little agreement on what exactly has gone wrong for America's youngsters and parents—let alone any consensus about what should be done. Rampant and growing child poverty is seen as the most pressing issue by many liberals, while for conservatives in both major parties the chief trouble lies in parental irresponsibility or the spread of divorce and unmarried motherhood. Whether government programs, actual or potential, help or hurt children is also a matter of fierce dispute. Conservatives see government "intrusion" and escalating or misdirected taxes as the culprits, while liberals focus on diminishing wages and public benefits.

In this chapter, we will consider liberal and conservative diagnoses about what is happening to American children and why. It won't take long to see that neither camp has a monopoly on wisdom and we are free to take valid insights from each side. Economic pressures and transformations in family structure both matter. Yet we need to take a much broader and longer term view of the difficulties faced by child-rearing families in America

103

than either today's liberals or conservatives tend to do.

Too much of today's debate focuses on issues about "welfare" and the situation of (just a fraction of) the very poor. Not enough attention is paid to the broadly similar dilemmas faced by single or dual working parents of modest as well as impoverished means. America needs to do more than just talk about children or debate poverty versus marital breakup as the cause of children's problems. We need to focus on working parents, the key actors struggling with new challenges in our time, and find ways to deliver more material and social support directly to those parents, so they can better nurture our children. In the process, we must reorient cultural messages and correct the inequities of national social programs that deliver a lot of support to families at the top and some help to those at the very bottom, while the majority of working parents have to struggle forward on their own.[5]

IS CHILD POVERTY THE PROBLEM?

The statistics about child poverty in the late-twentieth-century United States are indeed alarming—no matter which rendition of the numbers we consider. To begin, a cross-national perspective highlights how out of whack the country's current economic distributions may be. Americans are the best-off people in the world, if we consider not merely the incomes they enjoy but also the consumption goods they can afford.[6] No people in all of world history has been able to buy more stuff—houses, appliances, cars, clothes—or enjoy more services and diversions—restaurant meals, hairdos, movies, and vacations. Amidst all of this material abundance, though, the United States has an astounding rate of severe economic disadvantage for many of its children.

Scholars associated with the Luxembourg Income Study (LIS) have compared the economic situation of children across eighteen advanced industrial countries—fourteen European nations, plus Australia, Canada, Israel, and the United States—for the

1980s and 1990s.[7] The study was completed in 1995 (that is, prior to the 1996 "welfare reforms" in the United States, which many analysts believe could expose millions more children to deprivation, especially in an economic downturn). The LIS takes into account both wage incomes and governmental transfers and tax benefits, and defines poor children as those living in families with incomes less than 50 percent of the median income for all persons in each nation. The United States comes out with a much higher child-poverty rate than any of the other seventeen nations examined. Over one-fifth (21.5 percent) of U.S. children are poor, whereas child-poverty rates are under 10 percent in all European nations except Ireland (the poorest European country, with 12 percent of its children in poverty). As for other Western nations with child-poverty rates above 10 percent, the rates are about 11 percent for Israel and 14 percent for Australia. In short, despite great wealth, the United States has many more poor children than other Western nations, no matter how economically strong or weak those sister countries may be.

Some analysts suggest that U.S. children in poverty are nevertheless fairly well off (despite their relative deprivation compared to more privileged Americans). Of course poverty in a wealthy country is a much more liveable proposition than it is in destitute countries across the globe; but the issue here is how the United States compares to other industrial democracies. The Luxembourg Income Study examined the matter of the real standard of living of poor American families and compared it to the real standard for poor families in other Western nations, allowing for the fact that Americans overall can buy more with their nominal incomes. This comparison too underlines the depth of U.S. child poverty. Only two out of seventeen countries—Israel and Ireland, the two poorest nations in the study—have lower real standards of living for their impoverished children than the United States does for its poor children. As the LIS authors sum up, "while the United States has a higher real level of income than most of our comparison countries, it is the high and middle income children who reap the benefits (and much more the former than the latter). Low income American children suffer in both absolute and relative terms. The average low income child in the other 17 countries is at least one-third better off than is the average low income American child."[8]

Another way to look at U.S. child poverty is over time, especially since 1959, when official federal poverty rates started to be calculated for the national population and various subgroups within it.[9] Both older Americans and children used to experience a disproportionate share of poverty compared to working-aged adults; and as discussed in Chapter Three, the elderly of the 1960s and early 1970s were considerably *more* likely to be poor than were children at that time. But poverty trends shifted during the middle of the 1970s, when federal programs started to make a huge difference for the elderly. Poverty rates for Americans sixty-five and over plummeted, declining from one in three elderly persons in poverty around 1960 to about one in eight in poverty today (about the same poverty rate as for working-aged adults). Meanwhile, poverty rates for children came down a bit in the 1960s and early 1970s, but then resumed an upward climb. By now, more than one in five American children lives in poverty.

Deprivation is worst for the very youngest Americans—at a stage in life when poverty, as child development specialist James Garbarino explains, "can compromise a child's biological and psychological systems."[10] Arguably, too, deprivation has become more intractable. "Being poor becomes more and more a condition of life rather than an event in a family's history," says Garbarino, who points out that during "the 1960s, 32 percent of poor people in the United States moved out of poverty within a year of becoming poor; during the 1980s, only 23 percent experienced that same recovery."[11] Since the 1970s, both black and white poor families with children have had to subsist on incomes further and further below the official poverty line (with just a slight improvement since the middle of the 1990s).[12]

Economic Trends and Government Neglect

Why are there so many poor kids in America? To answer this question, liberal-minded analysts typically point to trends in the national economy since the 1970s that exacerbated shortfalls in governmental assistance to poor families with children.[13]

Since 1973, median real family income in the United States has stagnated in an era of slow national economic growth, while individual and family incomes alike have become much more unequal.[14] College-educated workers have seen their incomes grow, especially those in the top fifth of the national income distribution, but workers with high-school educations or less, especially men, have experienced actual declines in real wages. Many analysts point to this trend as a prime contributor to rising child poverty.[15] Back in the late 1950s, a high-school-educated father could make enough to sustain a family consisting of a homemaker mother and two children at an economic level above the poverty line. But that is much less likely to be true in the 1990s. The economic situation is even more desperate for a single-parent family whose head, usually the mother, has a high-school education or less.[16]

As we have seen, America's elderly have done well despite a slowly growing national economy and increasing economic inequality, and this has happened because the elderly have benefited from generous and modestly redistributive federal benefits, channeled through Social Security, Medicare, Medicaid, and Supplemental Security Income.[17] By contrast, American children have not enjoyed generous help through government. As the authors of the Luxembourg Income Study put it, "there is much less in the way of public support for both working and nonworking parents in the United States than is found in other nations," and this is what accounts for most of the greater poverty experienced by American children today.[18] Mother-led single-parent families tend to be pulled out of poverty by public programs in our sister democracies, but in the United States the real value of

AFDC and other means-tested welfare benefits has steadily eroded since the early 1970s; and anyway only about half of poor families were receiving such benefits in 1993.[19] The United States lacks the sorts of family or child allowances that are commonly found in other Western industrial nations—forms of governmental income transfers that do much to make up for the relatively meager incomes that low-income families can earn in the private marketplace.[20] Finally, in America many low-income workers either forgo—or pay extra for—vital family protections such as health insurance and child care that citizens of other advanced nations can take for granted.[21]

The Ambiguous Resonance of Child Poverty

Facts like these speak for themselves to many people. Child advocates, social service professionals, church leaders, and others who have championed public assistance for the needy are appalled at America's extraordinary rate of child poverty. They blame our national and state governments for not doing more to help poor children. Back in the 1980s and now again in the 1990s, say researcher-advocates such as Ruth Sidel in her tellingly entitled 1996 book, *Keeping Women and Children Last*, U.S. politicians have in effect "waged war" against the poor. A "campaign of vilification [is] being waged against poor women and children," Sidel writes, "a campaign that permits and legitimizes the destruction of remaining lifeboats in order to fuel the increasing wealth of the richest among us and to further the political fortunes of those in power."[22]

In 1996, when Congress and President Clinton decided to abolish federal guarantees of a minimum level of welfare provision (through Aid to Families with Dependent Children) for all poor youngsters in America, liberal child advocates reacted by sending thousands of telegrams and letters to officials saying "Shame on you for harming our children!" Child advocates believed that even-lower levels of public aid for the poor would result from pushing responsibility for public assistance onto the states and the (already economically desperate) cities. The results, liberal advocates envisaged, would be higher levels of family breakup and child neglect, swelling numbers of homeless children, more children going without food or new shoes or winter jackets, and increasingly desperate mothers who might turn to prostitution or drug-dealing when they could not find regular jobs sufficient to sustain themselves and their offspring. Liberals could not comprehend why it made any sense for America to take this course of action in the face of already appalling levels of child poverty.

But for others simple facts about child poverty may not carry the unequivocal message they do for liberal-minded researchers and advocates. There are various reasons why not everyone hears the same message. Conservatives opposed to "big government" may never want to hear information that suggests a need for expanded public activities. But there is more to it than that. Americans of modest means sometimes resent the focus that liberals place on the plight of the very poor. Hardworking parents in economically tight circumstances may feel that they and their own children suffer a lot of the same deprivations and constraints that are so often decried for the very poor. Racial and ethnic differences underlie some of the popular resentment, of course, but tensions exist among people of the same racial backgrounds, too.

Generational imbalances in U.S. social provision since the 1960s have heightened the potential for bitterness directed from the working middle class toward poor folks on the bottom. Publicly funded social supports for child-rearing families have mostly been means-tested "welfare" programs reaching only some of the very poor. Little has been done for other families with modest or low incomes, although this situation has improved somewhat through the Clinton administration's expansion of the Earned Income Tax Credit to reach more lower income working families.[23] Still, working families who are struggling economically but are not on welfare or eligible for Medicaid or generous child-care assistance can easily come to resent other, slightly less well-off families who *are* getting such public benefits. America's least well-off parents and children end up divided among themselves, popular fodder for warring politicians and ideologues. People may suspect that talk about "helping children" is really a cover for liberal efforts to protect or expand partial welfare programs.[24]

Another difficulty may lie in the ambiguous sense of what child poverty means—in contrast to the humanly vivid picture most people have when told about old people who are struggling economically. Older people, after all, are either living in their own households as independent adults, or else they used to be in that situation. When social statisticians speak of a poor elderly person, it is easy for members of the general public to picture and empathize with an old lady—someone like Michael Harrington's Louise W, perhaps—who is living out her days in a single room, pinching her pennies for halting walks to the supermarket. Or people can imagine an elderly couple trying to spread a fixed pension across groceries, prescription drugs, and heating bills. But when impoverished children are discussed, the translation of official statistics into human imagery is not so straightforward, because youngsters come attached to parents or other caregivers and do not live in separate households.[25] When any condition is mentioned for children, whether it be poverty or delinquency, people automatically wonder, "where are the parents?" Are the parents of these children behaving responsibly? If they cannot earn a good living, or control their offspring's behavior, why not?

Members of the general public also know perfectly well that governmental benefits to help children do not go directly to the children—not the way that most benefits intended for the elderly can go directly to the old men or women themselves, or else to the hospitals, doctors, and nursing homes that provide services directly to elderly clients. Where poor children are involved, public monetary benefits must flow through their parents, at least through their mothers; and the effectiveness of social services and supports typically depends on parental cooperation. This fact merely heightens public interest in what the parents are like, and what they are up to.

In short, for child advocates and others who work directly for and with the poor, the numbers—about poverty, or about declining levels of public aid—may speak directly and quite vividly in human terms. But the human message for the American public is not so clear-cut. The message is further muddied because liberals and conservative elites offer such strikingly different interpretations about the causes of America's extraordinarily high rates of child poverty.

ARE FRAGILE FAMILIES THE PROBLEM?

Poverty statistics may seem obvious to many, but social conservatives affiliated with both major political parties do not buy the liberal analysis. In their view, market processes and inadequate governmental benefits are not the primary reasons for child deprivation in late-twentieth-century America. Out-of-wedlock childbearing, divorce, and personal irresponsibility are the real culprits, conservatives say: there would be little poverty or social disruption for children if only men and women would get married before becoming parents and stay married while raising their offspring. This diagnosis has considerable popular resonance during an era when millions of men and women are perplexed by rapid changes in male-female relationships and the mounting challenges of combining paid work and parenthood.

On the hard right, the family breakup thesis has a blatant racial and misogynist edge to it. "The chief cause of black poverty is welfare state feminism" declares right-wing economist George Gilder in the *Wall Street Journal*.[26] "Thirty years of affirmative action programs have elevated black women into economic power over black men. . . . Welfare state feminism destroyed black families by ravaging the male role of provider." "Men," explains Gilder, "either dominate as providers or as predators. . . . The key problem of the underclass—the crucible of crime, the source of violence, the root of poverty—is the utter failure of the socialization of young men through marriage. The problem resides in the nexus of men and marriage. Yet nearly all the attention, subsidies, training opportunities, and therapies of the welfare state focus on helping women function without marriage." Charles Murray of the Manhattan Institute agrees with much of Gilder's analysis and worries that "underclass" problems are now spreading into the white population.[27] Mother-only families breed poverty, crime, and societal disintegration, and now low-income white women are having babies out of wedlock at about the rate that pertained for blacks two decades ago. Murray blames the situation mostly on female sexual promiscuity, arguing that if girls will not demand marriage in return for sex, men should not have to pay child support for out-of-wedlock children.

Gilder and Murray might be dismissed as extremists, but more moderate social conservatives focus on family fragility without the overtones of racism or misogyny. "[S]ocial issues drive economic data," argues Ben Wattenberg in his 1995 book *Values Matter Most*. "Family breakup is a very big reason why poverty rates aren't falling, stalled between roughly 12 and 15 percent for almost thirty years. It's a big reason why income inequality has increased, slowly, for several decades."

> In 1993, married-couple families with children under age eighteen had a poverty rate of *9 percent*. Families with a female head, no husband present, with children under age eighteen, had a poverty rate of *46 percent*! . . . The median income of a *husband-wife* family with children under age eighteen in 1993 was *$45,548*. For counterpart *female-headed* families, the median was *$13,472.*[28]

A "massive erosion of fatherhood contributes mightily to many of the major social problems of our time," agrees David Popenoe of the Council on Families in America.[29] "I am referring not only to the situation of the inner city poor . . . ," he stresses, "but to the overall quality of daily life."[30] Fathers are crucial to children's lives both economically and psychologically and, in Popenoe's view, married, two-parent families are one of the linchpins of decent modern societies. Yet "in just three decades, from 1960 to 1990, the percentage of children living apart from their biological fathers more than doubled, from 17 percent to 36 percent," and by the turn of the century nearly half of American children will not live with their fathers.[31]

Commentators who believe that family breakup is at the root of child deprivation can marshal their own appalling litany of contrasts between the United States and other advanced-industrial countries. Around 1960, over 90 percent of all American children were growing up with two parents. Because premarital pregnancies usually resulted in shotgun weddings, out-of-wedlock child rearing was very uncommon. And by mid-century U.S. children were no longer as likely as they earlier were to lose a parent to death. Even though the United States had long been the world's leader in divorce rates, the country went from 5 percent of marriages ending in divorce around 1900 to around 10 percent ending that way in 1960. "Up until the 1960s the lowering death rate and the increasing divorce rate neutralized each other as generators of single-parent families. . . . In 1900 the percentage of all American children living in single-parent families," mostly due to the death of a parent, "was 8.5 percent. By 1960 it had increased to just 9.1 percent," with more such children living with divorced mothers.[32] Hardly anyone worried about family fragility at that point, except perhaps as it affected African Americans.

But from then on, some extraordinary changes occurred in U.S. family structures and child-rearing arrangements. The proportion of children growing up with single parents (86 percent of whom are mothers) increased for a number of reasons. Married couples had fewer and fewer children, so in part the increasing "proportion" of children in single-parent families is due to the decline in births to two-parent families. Yet the U.S. divorce rate has also doubled over the past three decades. Despite some improvement in recent years, about half of all U.S. marriages currently end in divorce. And out-of-wedlock child rearing has skyrocketed, primarily because the nonmarital conception of a baby no longer leads to a wedding as it usually did in the America of the 1950s and earlier. "As late as 1965 only about one out of every thirteen births took place out of wedlock. Today, nearly one out of every three does. And just as divorce has overtaken death, nonmarital births are expected to surpass divorce as the leading cause of single-parenthood . . . later in the 1990s. Already today the proportions of single-parent children living with a divorced parent and a never-married parent are almost identical."[33]

Of course divorce, nonmarital childbearing, and single parenthood have all been on the rise across the advanced-industrial world, especially in Western societies. Nevertheless, the rate of single parenthood in the United States substantially exceeds that in all other developed nations: 23 percent of U.S children live in single parent families, while the proportion ranges from 11 to 17 percent in other Western democracies and is only 6 percent in Japan.[34] America's divorce rate is also well ahead of the rates in other advanced nations—although the United States is *not* the country with the highest percentage of births to nonmarried women, because certain other advanced nations have many non-married cohabiting parents.[35] Single-parent child rearing seems to be headed ever further upward in America, even as the divorce rate has dipped slightly.[36] As Sara McLanahan and Lynn Casper explain, the "higher prevalence of single motherhood in the United States is due in part to the fact that divorce is more common . . . and in part . . . [to the fact that] children born outside of marriage are less likely to live with both parents in the United States than in other countries."[37]

Increasingly fragile arrangements between the men and women who bear American children have obviously reduced the time that youngsters spend with both of their parents. By age seventeen, only about half of American children born between 1970 and 1984 were living with both natural parents, in contrast to "the nearly 80 percent figure of just three decades earlier." The situation seems even more "startling," as David Popenoe puts it, if one considers the rising proportion of childhood spent with only one parent. "White children born in the 1950–1954 period spent only 8 percent of their childhood with just one parent; black children spent 22 percent. Of those born in 1980, by one estimate, white children can be expected to spend 31 percent of their childhood years with one parent, and black children 59 percent."[38]

To be sure, quite a few children who cease to live with one of their natural parents (usually their father) end up with stepparents in the new "blended" families that are formed through remarriages. Although the U.S. rate of remarriage following divorce is going down steadily, most divorced women and men *do* marry again. In 1990, around 11 percent of children under eighteen lived with a stepparent.[39] But the situation for children in such "blended" families remains problematic.[40] Stepparents can have difficulty forming firm and caring relationships with stepchildren. And the rate of divorce for remarried couples is even higher than for first-married couples. So many children of divorce soon face another round of family instability, going through two, or even three, parental breakups—which are often accompanied by residential moves.

The Consequences for Children

So what? Does it matter much for children if they grow up— entirely, or for long stretches of their childhood—with a single parent, usually a single mother? In recent years, social scientists have compared children growing up in various kinds of families: two-parent families, remarried families, families headed by a divorced parent, and families headed by a parent who has never married. What circumstances do children face in these varied types of families, and how well do they do as teenagers and adults? The results of such research give considerable support to the claims of social conservatives: "Growing up with a single parent" does hurt children, concludes one of the best social science studies, a 1994 book with that title by sociologists Sara McLanahan and Gary Sandefur.[41] At the same time, some of the reasons *why* children experience different outcomes across various types of families are grounded in the economic realities that liberals stress.

Of course much of the difficulty for children with just one parent is economic.[42] Most single custodial parents are mothers, and a woman who tries both to earn a steady income and supervise her children finds life challenging at best. Many divorced mothers end up poor: "In 1991, 39% of divorced women with children lived in poverty, and 55% of those with children under six years of age were poor."[43] Even divorced custodial mothers who are not poor often experience sharp declines in income after the marital breakup. Things are still worse for the least-privileged women, whether divorced or never married. Those with limited educations are especially likely to have trouble finding steady jobs with good enough wages and benefits to sustain a family.[44]

Single mothers get insufficient help from the fathers of their children. After a divorce, children who stay with their mother may experience not only a squeeze of parental time and money; they may lose the family house, if it has to be sold to divide the proceeds between their parents. All too often, divorced fathers contribute very little to cover the costs of child rearing, still less to meet the costs of college. Divorced fathers are more likely than never-married fathers to be told by the courts to pay child support, but often these are only small payments until age eighteen. And a judicial award of support is not the same thing as the actual delivery of funds.[45] The performance of the child-support system has remained poor for a long time, with more than half of custodial mothers receiving no payments or less than the (already small) amounts legally ordered. It is little wonder that mothers raising children alone crowd the ranks of America's least economically secure families. The poorest of the poor, indeed, are single mothers with more than one child under six. Fully 77 percent of divorced single mothers in that situation, and 88 percent of unmarried single mothers with more than one young child, had incomes below the poverty line in the mid-1990s.[46]

The problems for children raised by single parents do not stop with economic deprivation. McLanahan and Sandefur deliberately looked at what happens to children in single-parent, step-parent, and dual-parent families in comparable economic circumstances, and their results document that offspring raised by single parents or stepparents are significantly more likely to drop out of school, get bad grades, become delinquent, or become pregnant as teenagers. The results are worse for children of nonmarital unions than for children of divorced parents.

Children in disrupted families are deprived of more than money, reason McLanahan and Sandefur. Such children are likely to have to change residences or communities and renegotiate significant human ties. They get less time and supervision from adults. And they do not have as many social networks—ties through both parents and their kin and friends—on which they can call as they move through childhood, schools, and into adult jobs. Sadly, most fathers who are not married and living with the mothers of their children tend to lose touch with their offspring. About 70 percent of divorced dads who are not remarried keep in some touch, but the contacts may be sporadic and superficial. Contacts drop off when divorced fathers remarry, or if many years have elapsed since the marital breakup; and men who were not originally married to the mothers of their children have less frequent contact than divorced fathers. A 1981 national survey found that "[f]ifty-two percent of all adolescents aged twelve to sixteen who were living with separated, divorced, or remarried mothers had not seen their fathers at all in more than a year, and only 16 percent saw their fathers as often as once a week."[47]

In short, empirical research confirms the social conservative insight that family fragility in America erodes the social fabric and hurts many children, both economically and developmentally. More and more children spend all or large parts of their youth with mothers alone. While many do well in life, a disproportionate number experience poverty; and whether poor or not, many children growing up in single-parent or remarried families experience extra difficulties at school, in the community, or in intimate relationships.

The Roots of Family Fragility

Why are there so many divorces, and why do so many mothers and fathers never marry at all? How has it come to be that increasing proportions of American children are born to unmarried mothers, or are being reared by caregivers other than two married parents? The reasons why such things are happening are crucial to our contemplation of how best to cope with new difficulties for children and their parents. But the causal answers offered by various brands of conservatives are not very compelling.

Activists in and around the antigovernment wing of the Republican Party proclaim that misbehaving poor people and federal welfare programs are the prime causes of family breakup and child suffering. The arguments of George Gilder and Charles Murray give a flavor of this analysis, and similar notions can be found in the political rhetoric of today's Christian Coalition or Congressional Republican leadership. Conservative Republicans have gotten a lot of antigovernment mileage out of crusades against "welfare" and underclass social misbehavior. But by any empirical standards, their ideas just do not hold up. Only 5.4 percent of Americans received AFDC benefits in 1993, and only one-third of poor families relied exclusively on welfare.[48] And that was before economic growth and the 1996 abolition of federal welfare guarantees trimmed the rolls drastically.

Not only are relatively few Americans "on welfare," but they have gotten less and less from such benefits during the period when worrisome family trends have unfolded. The value of all sorts of federal means-tested benefits, including food stamps as well as AFDC, started eroding in the 1970s, even as national rates of divorce and nonmarital childbearing went up. The fastest rate of increase in unmarried childbearing, moreover, is now occurring among college-educated women.[49] The causes of single parenthood in America are obviously much broader and deeper than federal programs for the poor.

Middle-of-the-road social conservatives are much more likely to blame legal and cultural transformations since "the sixties" for worrisome family trends. In *Life Without Father*, for example, sociologist David Popenoe considers economic, governmental, and cultural changes as possible causes of the overall declines in marriage and paternal commitment to children that he sees as so constitutive of U.S. social problems today. Welfare policies and diminished economic prospects for less educated men may account for some of the increase in nonmarriage and single parenthood among the very poor, Popenoe argues, but as "a general explanation for marriage decline in the American population as a whole, it is hard to see that the . . . government has played much role."[50] The large-scale entry of women into the labor force and the partial closing of the gap between women's and men's wages in the labor market may matter, because these recent labor-market trends make women more economically "independent" and slightly more able to get along without husbands. The movement toward "no fault" divorce laws—enacted across the U.S. states in the 1970s—also made marriages much easier to dissolve, Popenoe argues, and left custodial mothers with diminished resources of time and money to care for children. Yet Popenoe places the greatest emphasis by far on big transformations in culture and popular attitudes since the 1960s. Citing many sources, including findings by the pollster Daniel Yankelovich, Popenoe argues that Americans "today place a much lower value on what we owe others as a matter of moral obligation and a much higher value on self-realizing and personal choice."[51]

A shift away from social obligation and trust in institutions has occurred across all urbanizing and industrializing societies. America is "in the vanguard of this trend," however, because it is a culturally diverse society with a long-standing emphasis on individual achievement, and because it is a country where "con-sumption-driven wealth provides the wherewithal to pursue an individualistic lifestyle apart from the larger community."[52] "America currently seems to be spiraling toward an ever more unencumbered individualism," Popenoe argues, and marriage has been undermined. Marriage has become "much less a social insti-tution that expresses society's goals and more a personal, volun-tary relationship which individuals can make or break at will in their search for self-fulfillment."[53] Men, in particular, are likely to opt out of sustained commitments to marriage and children in a cultural atmosphere such as this.

Obviously, this sort of analysis leads toward rather different prescriptions than the hard-right formula blaming the "welfare state" for the unfortunate lives and prospects of many children. If broad transformations of culture and popular attitudes are encouraging a turn away from marriage on the part of Ameri-cans of all economic strata, then maybe restorative social changes can come only from intellectual and social movements, bolstered by legal adjustments. Many pro-family intellectuals are banding together in efforts to promote "communitarian" values, stressing social obligations. Some pro-family conservatives, including Democrats, also advocate regulatory steps: tax-code revisions to favor married couples who care for children at home, and revi-sions of marriage and divorce laws to make unions with children much harder to dissolve.[54] Realistically, such legal changes are unlikely to work in the absence of the broader cultural transfor-mations, reinforced by better material circumstances for married, child-rearing families. Indeed, new legal restrictions on divorce might actually backfire, if sexually active men and women were to become even more wary of marrying in the first place.

Populist "fatherhood campaigns" have also appeared in both the white and African American communities.[55] When hundreds of thousands of African American men joined the "Million Man March" in Washington, D.C., on October 16, 1995, responsible fatherhood was a major theme. Meanwhile, conservative Christian men, predominantly whites, have flocked to "Promise Keepers" rallies in football stadiums. They gather to hear speeches about family values, and then pledge to become responsible Christian "heads of households," more caring husbands and fathers. It is unclear what difference all of this makes, but such events and movements are surely a sign of popular concerns about family responsibilities and worries about the meaning of fatherhood. Although feminists rightly criticize pronouncements of male dominance occasionally made by leaders of the Promise Keepers and the Million Man March, these themes are only part of the story. For millions of men to participate in celebrations of fatherhood and the responsibilities of husbands to wives could end up, on balance, being a good thing for American society and for many women struggling to raise children and make ends meet.

Still, these are diffuse cultural revitalization movements that have touched only minorities of American men and families. Improvements in the conditions for child-rearing parents, married or not, certainly cannot rest only in the hands of those who attend Promise Keeper rallies or who went to Washington for the Million Man March. Or even in the hands of others who participate in smaller scale movements to enhance fatherhood. To the degree that social conservatives suggest that cultural movements alone, apart from public policies, can address the difficulties faced by American children and families, surely they are whistling in the wind.

Economic Changes and Fragile Families Both Matter

It doesn't take a Solomon to see it. Most Americans sense that arguments over political-economic "versus" social and cultural causes for child deprivation are artificial and misleading. Both macroeconomic shifts and new social tensions are clearly at work. Influences artificially polarized in ideological debates are thoroughly intertwined in daily life experience. What is more, the best social science shows that family transformations and economic trends have joined together to make life more difficult for most American families.

In their 1995 book *America Unequal,* social scientists Sheldon Danziger and Peter Gottschalk carefully estimated what proportion of increasing U.S. poverty after 1973 can be attributed to trends in the economy (slow growth, stagnant wages, and increasing income inequality) and what proportion can be attributed to shifts in family structure (principally the rise of single-parent families through divorce and unwed motherhood). It will not surprise any sensible person to learn that they discovered both sets of factors at work. Poverty in 1991, they conclude, was about 3.9 percentage points above what it would have been had there been no changes in family structure or economic inequality—in other words, if both the economic trends and family structures that underpinned the post–World War II American social economy had remained in place. "Our analysis shows," conclude Danziger and Gottschalk, "that about half the increase in poverty between 1973 and 1991 was due to rising [income] inequality; about 40 percent due to changes in family structure." Both rising economic inequality (even in periods of national growth) and the higher incidence of divorce and never-married parenthood are having an impact in late-twentieth-century America, throwing millions more children and parents (especially mothers) into poverty than would otherwise have been there.[56]

Similarly, in their 1996 compilation of social facts in *The State of Americans,* Urie Bronfenbrenner and his colleagues document many ways in which poverty and growing up with a single parent (especially both together) are associated with worrisome outcomes for children and young people.[57] A girl growing up with a single mom, for example, is very likely to become a single mom herself; and the risk of that outcome is much greater if her family of origin is also poor. The same sort of situation holds for risks of delinquency or doing poorly in school. Poor children, and children of single parents—often one and the same children—are least likely to complete high school or get college educations.

That is perhaps the most worrisome association of all, because educational achievement is becoming more and more important in late-twentieth-century America. It is hard to get a good job, with a substantial income and benefits, without a good education. So the problems of poverty and single parenthood, and both together, can easily become intergenerational traps.

Why should we choose either poverty or family fragility as problems for children, when they so obviously both matter in their own right and are often intertwined?[58] Common sense tells us that the proliferation of child-rearing families struggling to get by with the earnings and efforts of only one parent is bound to mean both more poverty and more disorganized lives for children, contributing to many other social ills. Common sense tells us that kids whose parents remarry usually have to move and work out new relationships, and may suffer loss of supervision as well as access to paternal resources. Common sense also says that eroding wages or economic downturns can contribute to family stress or breakup, or be an obstacle to marriages occurring in the first place. Families that cannot get by economically often fall into bitter quarrels, or worse, and these days either the man or the woman may just walk out.

Too much of the argument between liberals and conservatives has, in any event, been focused on very poor single-parent families. Between the mid-1960s and the mid-1990s, liberals focused on the very poor because Aid to Families with Dependent Children and other means-tested "welfare" programs were at the center of political controversy. Perhaps the economic distress does hit current or former "welfare mothers" and their children most severely, but millions of other single- and dual-parent families experience similar problems. The tight focus of policy debates on very poor single-mother-headed families has taken too much attention away from what is going on with the bulk of American families with children, those who are neither extremely poor nor in the top fifth of income earners. This is unfortunate even for the very poor, because economic possibilities and cultural standards for the very poor are profoundly influenced by what happens to those just above them in the class structure.

Not just the poorest, but the bulk of American men who are fathers already or who might become fathers are not likely to be able to earn enough wages and benefits to sustain a wife and children. Thus, two-worker families are proliferating along with solo-parent households. Families rely on two incomes (if husbands and wives can manage to stay together). "In 1960, 61 percent of all two-parent families managed on one income. In 1990, only 21 percent did."[59] The two-parent, dual-income family is arguably what most Americans consider normal, even ideal. And by the year 2000, estimates Donald Hernandez, more than four-fifths of all American children will be growing up in either two-parent-earner or single-parent-earner families—in sharp contrast to the situation as late as 1960, when more than half were growing up in male-breadwinner/female-homemaker "Ozzie and Harriet" families.[60]

The most startling transformation in recent decades has been the entry of married mothers of even very small children into the labor force. As Sara McLanahan and Lynn Casper explain:

Women's labor force participation—the percentage of women who are working or looking for work—has been going up since the beginning of the twentieth century. In the early part of the century the increase occurred primarily among young unmarried women. After 1940, married women began entering the labor force in greater numbers, and after 1960, married mothers with children at home followed suit.

In the early 1950s, only about 30 percent of married mothers with school-aged children were working outside the home. By 1990, this number had risen to over 73 percent. In just four short decades, a behavior that once described only a minority of mothers now fit a large majority of mothers, and this was true for mothers of all marital statuses. The figures for mothers with preschool children (under age 6) are even more dramatic. In 1960, only 19 percent of married mothers with preschool children were in the labor force, whereas by 1990, 59 percent were employed. By 1990, currently married mothers were nearly as likely to be in the labor force as formerly married single mothers (64 percent), and they were more likely to be employed than never-married mothers (49 percent).[61]

American men, meanwhile, are experiencing unsettling changes in economic prospects and social identities. During an era when female wages have risen, wages for less-educated men in the bottom two-thirds of the income distribution have stagnated or declined since the 1970s; and these earners also face eroding employer contributions to pensions and health care (and are often in jobs with no benefits at all).[62] The United States has gone from the era of breadwinner husbands and fathers to a time in which many never-married or divorced men live on their own, while most married men are co-earners with their wives (even in households with very young children). This is truly a brave new economic and cultural era for men, very unlike the world of their fathers and grandfathers who—ideally, if not always in reality—departed for work in the morning, leaving wives to tend homes and children.

Given the new economic and cultural relationships between men and women, if more and more men are avoiding family commitments or breaking away from those they have already taken on, then a significant part of the reason may be that many men cannot contribute enough economically to fulfill still deeply felt masculine ideals. Many less educated men really cannot earn enough; other men who do earn "enough" in some objective economic sense still find themselves contributing much less, relative to their female partners, than did the primary male "breadwinners" of the past.

Women, meanwhile, are still earning absolutely less than men—which means that many of the families they head will often be poor or nearly so. At the same time, American women on average are earning considerably more *relative to men* than they used to—mostly because women are putting much longer hours than before into paid employment, but also because women's wages have improved.[63] Before the 1970s, women's median wages tended to be about half of men's, but female median wages started moving upward in the 1970s, with the ratio of female to male wages "reaching 0.6 by 1989 and 0.65 by 1992. The ratio for full-time, full-year workers rose almost as much"—from about 0.6 before 1973 to about 0.7 in the early 1990s—"indicating that women's wage rates as well as their hours worked continued to increase after 1973. . . . Inequality between men and women has declined."[64]

For many child-rearing families, the new economic realities mean that (despite stagnation or erosion in male earnings) they can make it economically if two parents stay together and both work—especially if resources are heaped on one or two children. Indeed, in the top fifth of the U.S. income distribution, among professional, managerial, and business people, life can be downright materially luxurious for dual-earner couples. Part of the reason that family incomes are becoming more and more unequal in the late-twentieth-century United States is that the heights of the class structure are increasingly populated by pairs of highly educated men and women with at most one or two children. At all levels of income, however, two-parent families do much better on average than families that have to get by with the earnings of only one earner who is also a caregiver.[65]

Shifts in the balance of earning power between men and women accompany—and also partly cause—tensions that can prevent or break up marriages. The fact that women now do much more wage work and earn better incomes compared to the past may embolden them to avoid or break away from men who appear not to be pulling much weight. This same situation may sadden or irritate men who are concerned about their own earnings and market prospects. If it is true that millions of men and women in America today are finding it harder to get or stay married, then the unevenly changing economic prospects of men and women may be part of the reason why. This hypothesis seems all the more plausible when we realize that profound changes in personal identities and understandings of "the good life" are also tied up with changes in the gender composition of the labor market. What counts as men's or women's work has changed. So have our images of healthy and happy personal and family life.

Men still contribute about two-thirds of the income to dual-parent families, so their economic role is major for the most secure families. But women's incomes are vital too, not just for single-parent families, but also for two-parent families, most of which are now dependent on two incomes. This new situation for America's two-parent families can easily be a formula for lots of identity confusion and interpersonal conflict. He feels less in control than before, and more pressured to take on household and child-rearing duties. She, meanwhile, is working "double shift" in the wage market and the household, where she is still doing most of the housework and child rearing. Is it so surprising that many women can end up being irritated with men who seem insufficiently helpful, while many men can end up thinking life would be more fun on their own, or in a new marriage?

Such tensions end up being more acute among people with lesser educations, incomes, and economic prospects.[66] In all societies at all times, family ties are most fragile among the economically least privileged. In the United States today, moreover, tensions between men and women are greatest among African Americans, who face special cultural contradictions and economic difficulties.[67] Black women have a long history of combining wage earning with child rearing, while many black men want to be traditional breadwinners but struggle in schools and labor markets. Nevertheless, economic tensions and clashes of identity and aspiration between men and women are happening among all groups of Americans these days. So it makes little sense to talk about poor men and women, or blacks in particular, as if they were in a completely different situation from everyone else.

They aren't, because many of the same economic trends matter across the income structure, and because nonmarital childbearing and divorce and decisions to rear children outside of marriage are climbing upward among all groups of Americans.

Too often the discussion of "factors" that promote poverty and family breakup is excessively statistical and antiseptically impersonal. But in real lives, the processes come together in poignant ways. In March of 1994, the *New York Times* ran a moving story about the Craig and Susan Miller family of Overland Park, Kansas, weaving together facts about America's changing job and wage structures with a specific story about one man and his workmates.[68]

Craig Miller was a thirty-seven-year-old married father of four children who had lost his former $15.65-an-hour job as a sheet metal worker for Trans World Airlines. "When he began to search for another job, he quickly learned the market value of a blue-collar worker with a strong back and a good work ethic but few special skills: about $5 an hour."

To earn about $18,000 a year, less than half what he formerly took home from T.W.A., Craig and his wife Susan juggled four jobs between them, his flipping hamburgers at McDonald's, driving a school bus, and (not very successfully) trying to launch a small installation business; hers stocking shelves nighttimes at Toys R Us. For eighteen hours a day, the Millers alternated between work and care for their four children, one of whom was learning disabled and doing well only with sensitive and skilled help from his local school. Because of that, the Millers did not feel they could move, despite the dawn-to-dusk grind of their lives as low-wage working parents, and despite the indignity Mr. Miller felt working at McDonald's.

> As the Millers gaze into the future . . . they see an employment landscape shaped like a barbell. At one end are bankers and lawyers and accountants exulting in the high-flying stock market; at the other end are countermen at fast-food franchises and clerks

at big discount stores struggling to pay the bills. The solid, working-class middle ground, where the Millers once stood, has meanwhile grown quite narrow—and slippery.[69]

Many of Craig Miller's buddies from his former T.W.A. job had also experienced layoffs, and we also glimpse a bit of their fate in the *Times* article. Other stories are much sadder than that of the Millers, but they shed light on the many ways in which the economic stresses of our era can directly contribute to personal disintegration and family failures.

> One of the men, Joe Tomczuk, could not find a job that paid more than $6 an hour. He moved back home with his parents, at age 39, and wondered if he should abandon the hope of ever getting married and starting a family.
>
> "Women are just like me; they want security," Mr. Tomczuk said. "What are they going to see in me?"
>
> Another former colleague [of Craig Miller's] is now a janitor in a school. Others seem to have disappeared.
>
> In the months after T.W.A. laid off several hundred workers like Mr. Miller, some marriages collapsed. Alcohol took a toll. And union officials say perhaps a dozen men peered into the blackness of the future and committed suicide.[70]

Finishing this article, one is left with a quiet sense of awe about Craig Miller. How many married men, one wonders, would stick it out so patiently with their families under these circumstances? Susan Miller seems remarkably steady, too—although she was not optimistic about the future. "'For people like us,'" she told the *Times* reporter, "'I'm afraid the good times are gone for good.'"[71]

A SOCIETY THAT UNDERCUTS PARENTS

Not only are public debates about social policy today excessively focused on very poor families, ignoring what is happening to people like the Millers. The debates often miss what may be the central point: The United States in the late twentieth century has become a society that devalues and undercuts parenthood—even more than it may undercut marriage.[72] The burdens the Millers face are very telling in this regard. Their struggles in today's economy are made all the more difficult because they are caring for four children, including one who needs stability in a specific environment. Craig and Susan Miller are not unencumbered free-market actors, and the privations they face are worsened by their steady commitment to the well-being of their children.

Marriages are fragile today, but the institution itself continues. Americans, after all, remain one of the "most marrying" people in the world, even if more adults than in the past remain unmarried, and even if divorce is prevalent. Most divorced men and women soon remarry. However, the proportion of families with children in the U.S. population has contracted sharply in recent decades. Almost 57 percent of all American families had children under age eighteen back in 1960. By 1996, the proportion had dropped to 49 percent.[73] America is more and more a society of single persons living alone and households of married couples without children. Of course, many married-couple households once had children, or plan to have them in the future. But there are also a lot of married couples who have not had children, or will not have them.

So the proportionately fewer American families who are raising children are doing a more vital job for all of us. As prominent economist Victor Fuchs puts it, children are a "public good."[74] The nation's cultural and economic future—and the affordability of its social benefits for the elderly, too—depends on the development of healthy, well-educated, and responsible young people.[75] Today's children will be the workers, parents, and citizens of tomorrow. With fewer children for each family to worry about—and fewer children for the nation as a whole—it ought to be easier to do a better job of raising them. Certainly, it is vital to do a good job. But, alas, many circumstances in the

United States are converging to make it harder for parents to raise children, not easier.

There are some bright spots, of course. Because child-rearing families tend to be smaller in the late-twentieth-century United States than they were up through the 1950s, each child can potentially get more support.[76] Research shows that parents with one or two children can "invest" more in them, so youngsters from smaller families do better on average. In addition, the educational level of parents has been shown to matter a lot for children's well-being and future success. Adult Americans have attained steadily more education over the past half century. So most youngsters today have parents who finished at least high school. "Children living with a parent with a high school diploma or higher went up from 62 percent in 1970 to 80 percent in 1990. This has translated into better educational attainment among children. . . ."[77]

But if we turn to other factors that influence how readily and well parents can raise children, the situation is not so bright. Consider the overall U.S. economic context from a parental perspective. Both average and median incomes for families with children have lost ground over the past several decades in America, compared to average and median incomes for families with no children under eighteen. This is not just due to higher poverty rates for families with children—serious as that increase has been—but also attributable to a growing economic disadvantage faced by adult men and women who commit themselves to children. As economist Fuchs puts it, the "weak economic position of children becomes readily apparent when households are grouped according to the presence of children. Money income per person is twice as high in households without children; and the more children in the household, the lower the income on average."[78] Of course there are some economies of scale for households, but Fuchs concludes that the economic deficit for child-rearing families remains even when these savings are factored into the equation.

The average cost of raising a child from birth to age eighteen in middle-class America today is over $150,000—not counting what may be needed to put a child through college.[79] In a society that is increasingly "monetized"—that is, where money is needed to buy most of the goods and services people need—parents have to raise the resources to feed, shelter, clothe, educate, and entertain children pretty much on their own, from their own wages and salaries, unless they are very wealthy or have well-to-do parents who help them. Yet American parents are struggling with the expenses of child rearing in an overall national economy generating wages not growing as much as many child-rearing expenses, where houses and apartments have become more expensive, and where employers have been steadily pulling back on many family-relevant benefits, such as health insurance. The media today gives a lot of attention to employers who offer flextime or extra benefits to parent-workers. Such employers are indeed worth celebrating, but they are a tiny minority; they mostly deal with well-paid workers; and they are counterbalanced by the growing ranks of employers who are offering low-wage jobs with few or no benefits.

U.S. families with children not only face tighter economic circumstances than childless couples and individuals. The time squeeze for parents is even more dramatic. Raising children is, inescapably, something that requires concentrated blocks of time and attention. But the entry of more and more wives and mothers into the wage-labor force, and the increasing hours that women in the labor force are on the job, has left both single-parent and dual-earner families with a lot less time for household work, child rearing, and community involvements (many of which revolve around children). According to Fuchs, household time available to children went down sharply from 1960 to 1986. "On average, in white households with children parents had ten hours less per week of potential parent time; the decline for black households with children was approximately twelve hours per week."[80] Other analysts calculate an even steeper decline in parental time from 1960 through the middle of the 1980s; and recent labor-market trends have taken even more time away from parenting. In a 1996 survey conducted for the National Parenting Association, overwhelming proportions of moms and dads alike were in the paid-labor force, and a fifth of the parents reported "holding two or more jobs in order to earn enough money to maintain a reasonable standard of living."[81] As economist Juliet Schor, author of *The Overworked American*, explains, between the 1960s and the 1990s, the average American couple has added the equivalent of another half-worker job per year, taking the hours out of time that used to go for children, leisure, and time for women to sleep.[82] In addition, more and more American children, even in dual-parent families, are finding themselves left alone—in what is called "self care"—at least for a time after school each day.

Single-parent families often face the toughest time-allocation dilemmas, especially if it is a mother trying to both take home a paycheck and care for her children. Safe, cheap child care is often not available; and single working moms may end up living in dangerous neighborhoods, where even their older children really need supervision after school. Part-time work might be the best answer for poor single mothers, and in fact most moms on AFDC were working at least part-time off the books while collecting benefits. But in the wake of the abolition of Aid to Families with Dependent Children in 1996, there will be more and more pressure on "welfare mothers" to do paid jobs virtually full-time. Thus, parental time may well shrink still further for the very families that are most vulnerable to pitfalls for unsupervised youngsters.

American parents know that they are in a bind. In a 1991 Gallup poll, two-thirds of working parents reported a feeling that they spend too little time with their children. Perhaps not surprisingly, three-quarters of working women said they feel torn between employment and family responsibilities, with 73 percent saying that they "wish they could stay home and be a homemaker sometimes."[83] And 82 percent of the fathers and mothers responding to the 1996 National Parenting Association survey believe they are having a harder time balancing work and family responsibilities than their parents did.[84]

As Juliet Schor eloquently argues, America's on-demand employment system has a lot to do with the time squeeze Americans, and particularly the "encumbered" parents among us, now face. U.S. corporations and unions developed their career patterns and expectations for employee achievement during the middle of the twentieth century, when the male-breadwinner/female-homemaker family was the primary site for child rearing and community engagements. Adult men were expected to work long hours, week after week, raising the family income, while their wives tended to homes, children, and community work. But then, starting in the 1960s, and accelerating with the onset of slow national economic growth in the 1970s, family structures became more fragile and male breadwinners ceased to be able to sustain middle-class family life. Wives and mothers entered the labor force for more and more hours per week, and more and more weeks during the year. Amidst all of this, Schor writes, employers kept long-standing expectations about "good workers." A committed employee is still supposed to act like a male breadwinner once did. Females and dual-parenting men are supposed to fulfill the old expectations, being available on demand to meet employer expectations, working at least forty-hour weeks, and perhaps more for "overtime" pay.

Employers who demand more and more from workers are not only responding to competitive market pressures without due attention to new family realities. As Schor points out, America's antiquated laws make the situation worse. Many U.S. labor laws were passed back in the 1930s and 1940s to define part-time and full-time jobs and set requirements about overtime pay or employer-provided benefits. In contrast to the situation in many European countries, U.S. work rules create incentives for employers to work "full-time" workers harder, while also proliferating part-time or temporary jobs without family-relevant benefits like health insurance. To avoid hiring new workers and giving them benefits, employers have an incentive either to hire temps or to give, or demand, overtime—which many workers want in order to make ends meet in an era of stagnating or declining real wages.

Had U.S. trends in the reduction of normal workweeks from 1900 to 1940 continued, Schor estimates that the average "full-time" workweek would now be 35.5 hours. But instead many workers, especially men, are putting in time and a half or working two or three jobs; or else two workers in one family are over-committed together. Schor believes that dual-worker families should contribute no more than thirty hours of wage work apiece, leaving time for child rearing, community, and leisure activities. But to achieve this norm would require major changes in goals and workplace practices on the part of government, employers, and unions alike.

Another part of the equation is America's intensely consumerist "earn and spend" economy.[85] As adults put more and more time in at work, they naturally buy more and more restaurant meals and personal services. But people also feel they have to buy a lot of goods—to be happy, to keep up with others, to fulfill images of success through possessions that appear everywhere. More than their counterparts in any other rich country, U.S. adults and children are deluged with invitations to buy things. There are incessant advertisements on television. Everywhere, shopping malls are virtual community centers—and hangouts for teenage children. If a household has a decent income, the phones ring nightly offering new credit cards. Credit cards come in the mail. And when he was eight years old, my son found a "play" credit card in a child's frozen dinner. Advertisers know that catching them young is the key to attracting consumer dollars from the teen years on.

Because there are so many consumer "needs," putting in extra time at work to earn the incomes to buy things seems natural in late-twentieth-century America. The consumerist economy nicely complements the practices of employers. And if children are left to watch TV while their parents work, that may only intensify the very consumer desires that incomes must satiate. This is much of what David Popenoe must mean when he talks about changing American values. But notice that definitions of success and personal happiness through individual wealth are hardly developing apart from the economy and governmental rules of the market game.

The value of parenting in America is just as profoundly influenced by new economic realities and cultural trends as the stability of marriage (David Popenoe's chief focus). If both men and women are supposed to work for wages and pursue career success—and if purchasable possessions, services, and opportunities for entertainment are endlessly available and defined as vital to "success" or "happiness"—the value of children is bound to be affected. Either children become the ultimate way to display success and consumption, or they become a drag, bound to keep adults (whether married or not) from being as "happy" or "successful" as they might otherwise be.

We see both outcomes in contemporary America. Some parents treat their children as emblems for display, as the parents of the murdered six-year-old Colorado girl, JonBenet Ramsey, did when they dressed her in adult-looking outfits and paraded her around to beauty pageants. Materialistic child display usually takes more subtle forms. Perhaps rich parents are proud of their kid's private education, good grades, and acceptance to Harvard, so they reward Johnny with a new car, or Sally with a summer vacation in Italy between high school and college—making very sure that their neighbors and social peers know about both the successes and the rewards, which reflect so well on the "successful" parents. Or a different version of the consumption-display scenario may play itself out in an inner-city ghetto, when a young unmarried mom dresses her baby in the fanciest possible outfit and the proud young father drops in every few months with an expensive present.

Other young people and adults have a more go-it-alone understanding of wealth, consumer display, and success. They avoid having children at all—or else father them, and then leave. In the ghetto, the unwed father may move on to a new girlfriend and spend his money on leather jackets. In the middle-class suburb, the divorcing dad may stop child-support payments so he can afford a new apartment and car—and perhaps a new wife. But it amounts to very much the same thing. For more and more American adults, the pursuit of happiness may mean the avoidance of costly and time-consuming commitments to children.

Intertwined economic and cultural pressures conspire to push adult Americans in one or another of these two directions. Children today do tend to be understood by Americans as private tastes. If people choose to have children, many think it is their "own affair"—and "private responsibility." "They shouldn't do it unless they can afford it," the popular saying goes—much as "they shouldn't buy a car unless they can cover the payments." Other citizens who do not "choose" to have children should not have to pay for welfare, or contribute to health benefits for families with children, or pay taxes for schools. Why should they have to pay the freight for "other people's children"? Attitudes such as these are very much abroad in the land.

At present, little in U.S. public debates or policy gives real force to the alternative possible way for Americans to look at children—as the future of the whole society. Back in the 1950s, the U.S. tax system favored married couples with children and afforded a degree of protection to household work outside of the paid economy.[86] But thereafter—until the very recent expansion of the Earned Income Tax Credit and some child-care tax credits—federal taxes encouraged market investments and individual market activity, providing dwindling shelters for child-rearing families. Existing U.S. social benefits are skewed toward the retired elderly. And they place heavy payroll tax burdens on young families, without giving full credit toward retirement benefits for time spent on child rearing as opposed to waged employment.

It would be a mistake, to be sure, to downplay the help that U.S. parents with children indirectly get from Social Security and Medicare. More than a quarter of Social Security recipients are spouses or children of retired, deceased, or disabled workers.[87] And things would be much worse for middle- and low-income American families with children if they simultaneously had to cover grandparents' needs for income and health care. Since the GI Bill, however, the most costly and inclusive U.S. social programs have not done much to help the majority of working-aged parents and children. One significant exception is the Earned Income Tax Credit (EITC), which uses refundable tax credits to significantly boost the incomes of near-poor working men and women. This measure, however, ties family well-being closely to wage work by parents. And the EITC cannot make up for the absence of paid family leaves, employer-pensions, or public or private health insurance for many low-wage workers.

During the 1990s there has been a lot of political rhetoric about children and families. But Americans have the right to take all the talk with a grain of salt, because too little is actually being done—by employers or by government—to make life significantly better for hardworking parents of modest or humble means. Liberals may talk about "our children," but they often advocate help only for "the poor," and have lately concentrated on delivering social services to children apart from their parents. Liberals too often cede the agenda to conservatives—who talk about helping "the American family" yet stress the exclusive responsibility of each set of parents for its own offspring. Worse, conservatives in both major parties advocate practical legislative steps that will leave most American families with children in even tougher economic and cultural circumstances than they now are, while delivering economic windfalls to the wealthiest third of households.

At the end of the twentieth century, in short, major U.S. institutions do not really convey the message that our nation has a shared stake in the work of parents and the well-being of all children. Some leaders in the private and public sectors may talk the talk about helping children and families. But the organizations over which they preside do not walk the walk—not when it comes to delivering real support for the efforts of ordinary child-rearing families, not when it comes to honoring the work of parents as much as the dollars of consumers or the hours put in by employees.

The time has come to do better. Americans *can* preserve the hard-won security of our grandparents, while fashioning an array of social supports offering greater security and opportunity to all parents—and, through them, to their children. As we are about to see, more than new "policy proposals" will be needed. A family-friendly America depends on the revitalization of our democracy as well as the reorientation of our national social policies. America's civic life and politics need to change if we are to become a nation with genuine family values.

CHAPTER FIVE

*Reaching for the
Middle: What It
Will Take to Build
a Family-Friendly
America*

DURING THE SUMMERS my family lives in Maine, where my son attends day camp with other children from a broad cross section of the community. At events for the kids, parents naturally fall to talking—and I vividly remember one conversation during the summer of 1994 at my son's day camp.

It was August, and yearlong national and Congressional debates over comprehensive health care reform were coming to a climax. On the nightly news, President Clinton and Congressional Democratic leaders were still talking as if something major might pass before Congress recessed in September. As the children enjoyed ice cream and games, I sat on a picnic table and chatted with Annemarie McAndrew, the mother of Jeffrey, a friend of my son Michael.[1] This was the first time I had met Annemarie. She usually couldn't come to Jeffrey's day camp, because—as she now explained—she worked a long shift as a health aide at a nursing home one town away. She had once been on welfare, she said, and was glad to be able to work now. She explained that Jeffrey's grandmother usually watched his sister and him after school or camp, until she could get home. As we talked, Annemarie recounted a recent emergency where they had to rush Jeffrey in an ambulance to the hospital. She was still trying to pay that off. She didn't have health insurance at her job, and Maine's bare-bones public coverage for the kids would not cover an ambulance, or any other extras. She spoke bitterly about her former husband, who had walked out on her and left her holding the bag. She was very grateful for her mother-in-law's constant help, though. Her mother-in-law owns her own home and she probably receives Social Security (I did not stop the flow of conversation to ask such an explicit question). Annemarie's mother-in-law is devoted to her two grandchildren. Her help and nearby residence has made it possible for Annemarie to get by in a demanding low-wage job.

To have something hopeful to say amidst all of this, I mentioned the Clinton administration's plan to guarantee "health care that's always there" for all Americans. "Maybe something will soon happen in Washington to help out with the health care," I offered, explaining just a bit about Clinton's Health Security proposal and the maneuvering around it. Annemarie listened politely and responded in a kindly tone, yet unmistakably looked at me as if I had just arrived from the moon. "Nothing they do there"—meaning Washington, D.C.—"ever makes any difference for people like me," she replied, putting a firm end to that phase of our conversation.

Annemarie was right, of course. Within weeks, the great 1993–94 debate over universal health care fizzled out into no Congressional action at all. President Clinton never even gave a speech stressing the enormous loss he—and the Annemaries of America—had suffered. And he has never again taken up the fight for universal health coverage. When Congress got around to enacting piecemeal reforms during 1995 and 1997, tiny steps were presented as huge breakthroughs but did not extend health insurance to low-income workers like Annemarie. Some other recent changes might help her children, but probably only partially and only if Annemarie is prepared to handle a lot of bureaucratic maneuvering and paperwork. Congressionally enacted "health reforms" applicable to adults have been regulations helpful to people who can afford to pay private insurance premiums or are covered by employer-provided insurance. Meanwhile, the ranks of the uninsured, crowded with Americans who work for modest wages and their children, continue to grow inexorably by about another million each year.[2]

Some of the things Congress has done, or might do, about Medicare, Medicaid, and Social Security could make Annemarie's situation still worse—worse when she eventually retires with little income to fall back on; and worse even sooner, if nearby local health centers end up closing or if Annemarie's mother-in-law is adversely affected. Annemarie may turn out to be lucky if "nothing they do there ever makes any difference," because many moves currently pushed by advocacy groups, pundits, and conservative politicians of both parties could easily harm Americans like her. Things could also deteriorate for struggling two-parent families like the Craig and Susan Miller family of Overland Park, Kansas, that we briefly encountered in Chapter Four.

As the new century arrives, Americans of good will need to transform our civic life and politics so people such as Annemarie McAndrew and Craig and Susan Miller are at the center—not off the edge—of our national systems of social support. It really is not good enough to extend health care and a scattering of other benefits to some of the children of adults who work for modest wages, leaving the parents themselves out in the cold. Adapting to a politics-as-usual, inhospitable to major new initiatives, many liberals have concluded that helping children is the best we can do. But ignoring working adults—above all working parents—is ethically obtuse and politically dumb. This approach will not build the moral and political foundations to make the changes America really needs.

Adults are the ones who vote; and they are the ones who must care for children. All of us who fly in airplanes are accustomed to the standard safety message about the oxygen masks: "If the mask drops down and you are traveling with a child, put your own mask on first and then help the child." This makes good sense, we realize, because children need their parents to be in good shape, fully functional. The same is true in our economy and communities. Children need healthy parents who can earn a living, care for them, and participate in community and national decisions on their behalf. Benefits or services administered by social service professionals are not an acceptable substitute for strong and caring parents. Americans agree that parents should be able to do their jobs—at home and in the community, as well as in the workplace.[3] So there are bright prospects for a new progressive politics focused on social supports for all working parents—especially if actual parents are included as responsible citizen-partners, not just as "clients."

How can American politics be recentered to reach adults as well as children in the missing middle? It won't happen simply because policy intellectuals outline technically detailed proposals. And it won't happen through marginal bipartisan adjustments among dominant stakeholders in Washington—not given the realities of contemporary electoral politics and top-down advocacy politics. In electoral politics and beyond, there must be a new popular mobilization by and for ordinary American families. Working parents should be at the center of this mobilization, although they cannot be—and should not be—the only ones involved. The entire country has a stake in better support for working parents.

Reaching for the missing middle in American politics requires both a bold vision of the cultural ideals and social supports we want to maintain and create, and a hard-nosed strategy for arousing new energy to push in that direction. Americans can reconnect with—and revitalize—our best traditions of democratic social provision. That means keeping in mind what has worked well, again and again. America thrives with social policies that bridge class and other social divides. The best social programs offer individuals and their families supports in return for contributions to the larger community; and they are nurtured by partnerships between government and citizens' associations. Again

143

and again, the United States has created generous and effective social supports following this formula. We can find ways to do it again—this time with working parents at the epicenter of our efforts.

BUILDING A FAMILY-FRIENDLY AMERICA

What might a refurbished system of family supports look like? This is not the place for arcane policy details, but we can imagine what might be desirable. Possible improvements are ready to hand, because experts and civically active groups have already suggested many ways to sustain and improve America's existing social insurance programs, while improving our supports for working families. Too often, though, policy proposals are discussed as technical plans in isolation from one another. If promising ideas are to become more than rhetorical gestures in election-year speeches, they must be connected to an overarching agenda and strategy. Americans will be much more likely to support specific steps if people understand how each measure contributes to a society where all working men and women can support their families, contribute to the nation, and enhance opportunities for our children.

The Best Defense Is a Good Offense

As we learned in Chapters Two and Three, conservatives are campaigning to cut back and break up America's largest inherited social insurance programs, Social Security and Medicare. During the 1980s and 1990s, antigovernment Republicans and market-oriented advocacy groups have taken advantage of new demographic and fiscal circumstances to provoke public anxiety about the expense and long-term viability of both of these federal programs. The generational imbalances that became so apparent in U.S. social provision after the 1960s allowed critics to argue that payroll taxes and "entitlement spending" for the elderly are "unfair" to the young; and the huge federal budget deficits of the

1980s allowed fiscal watchdogs to claim that Social Security and Medicare were propelling the nation toward "bankruptcy" or exorbitant levels of taxation.

Attacks on social insurance made headway. In the face of rising health care costs and an expanding elderly population, cuts in Medicare spending were used in 1995 and 1996 to help balance the federal budget. Now many Republicans and conservative Democrats advocate the elimination of Medicare's guaranteed benefits to the elderly on terms that would allow private insurers to lure the healthiest and wealthiest retirees away from broad insurance pools.[4] Meanwhile, critics of social insurance use the booming stock market to argue for individualistic alternatives to Social Security, suggesting that younger Americans can "do better" by investing (all or a portion of) payroll taxes in personal accounts managed by Wall Street brokers.

Preoccupied with battles about welfare, universal health insurance, and aid to poor children, supporters of public social provision in the United States were slow to realize that Social Security and Medicare were in political danger. Liberals long took these programs for granted as the "third rail" of American politics, presuming they were so popular that politicians who touched them would die. Liberals stopped making moral arguments about social insurance and relied upon backstage technical adjustments to keep taxes and projected benefits in long-term balance. This line of defense faltered when conservatives mounted public attacks on "entitlements," but progressives did not quickly respond. By 1996 and 1997, it looked as if people pushing to restructure Social Security might achieve a partial diversion of payroll taxes into millions of tax-advantaged Wall Street accounts. As I have already argued, such "partial privatization" would be the beginning of the end for an inclusive and redistributive Social Security system, because privileged Americans would agitate to expand individual accounts and cut taxes flowing into the shared retirement system. Yet many Republicans and "new Democrats" are prepared to accept partial privatization as a supposed compromise between the existing Social Security system and the complete individualization of retirement savings.

At the eleventh hour, as some Clinton administration planners showed signs of embracing the partial diversion of Social Security payroll taxes into individual investment accounts, progressives woke up and began to argue and mobilize on behalf of shared Social Security. Supported by liberal think tanks and advocacy groups, the feisty AFL-CIO led the way during 1998, pressuring elected officials and waging a broad campaign of popular education to remind union members—and many other Americans as well—why Social Security is both morally legitimate and vital to the material well-being of most retirees. This argument fell on fertile ground because privatization schemes are potentially very costly to taxpayers and beneficiaries, and the vast majority of Americans have a strong stake in Social Security's dignified, guaranteed, and slightly redistributive promised benefits.

Pushed by the newly aroused defenders of Social Security, President Clinton decided to endorse shared approaches to reform in his January 1999 State of the Union message. Supporters of social insurance breathed a nationally audible sigh of relief when the president called for "saving Social Security and Medicare" and advocated devoting most projected future federal surpluses to shoring up the finances of these programs. The "best way to keep Social Security a rock-solid guarantee," declared Clinton, "is not to make drastic cuts in benefits . . . and not to drain resources from Social Security in the name of saving it." Hoping to steal the march from advocates of private investments, Clinton proposed that a portion of accumulated Social Security taxes should be collectively invested in market securities to increase the rate of return for all future retirees. He also suggested a new, separate system of individual "USA Accounts," to be subsidized by the federal government in ways that would favor low-to-modest income earners.

But supporters of social provision cannot afford to relax. President Clinton's proposals can be compromised or whittled away in Congress. Joined by many conservative Democrats, Republicans will push to dismantle Medicare's guarantees. And Republicans are opposed to socially managed Social Security investments in the stock market. Congressional Republicans will try to rework Clinton's proposed "USA Accounts" to divert funds and support from Social Security. In short, 1999 and 2000 will see continuing battles about the future of Social Security and Medicare.

Now that the federal budget "crisis" has been declared over, conservatives do not want to use projected surpluses for broad social programs. They want to cut taxes instead. For many Republicans, across-the-board cuts are the ideal, even though they would deliver the greatest benefits to families making $100,000 a year or more. Conservative and moderate Democrats prefer more targeted tax cuts and credits. Either way, projected future "surpluses" could quickly dwindle, becoming insufficient to cover future retirees—and equally unavailable to meet additional pressing needs for elderly and young Americans.

Supporters of broad and inclusive social provision must, therefore, keep parrying threats to the structure and financing of existing programs. But the best defense of the core principles and shared revenue pools of Social Security and Medicare may require a good offense, not just an attempt to preserve the status quo. Because there really are marked generational imbalances in U.S. social provision, many needs of working-aged Americans and their children remain unmet. As conservatives press to dismantle shared insurance for the elderly, the best response may be to increase the stake of people of all ages—and generations—in national social programs. The art of politics is figuring out proposals that help to build broad political alliances.

President Clinton's proposals for "saving Social Security" meld a defense of the shared system with gestures toward pro-market forces. Technically acceptable as Clinton's ideas might be— assuming they can be implemented—they are hardly bold moves. Instead of gesturing toward Wall Street, why not find ways to bridge the needs of older and younger Americans as existing retiree programs are modified for the future? Social Security already includes disability and survivors insurance, both of which protect large numbers of vulnerable Americans under age sixty-five.[5] Yet there are excellent possibilities to extend the stake of working-aged families in social insurance.

One way to turn Social Security into a "generational alliance," as economist Barry Bluestone puts it, involves using current surpluses to finance improved education and training for American workers, including parents who seek to improve skills while caring for children.[6] Although the Social Security Trust Fund—the accounting of accumulated payroll taxes—will eventually have more charges against it than credits, it will remain in surplus for a couple more decades. In the meantime, the Trust Fund could finance GI Bill–style loans to post–high-school students and working adults who need retraining to keep up with today's fast-shifting labor-market opportunities. The possibility of combining training with part-time parenting could be included in the loan program. As Bluestone has outlined in detail, training loans could boost the career prospects and incomes of many younger Americans, who could then repay the loans from their future earnings. Calibrated to each individual's wages over several decades following the use of the loan, the debts to the Social Security Trust Fund could be collected through automatic payroll deductions—just like Social Security taxes are—thus minimizing defaults. To create a win-win situation both for working-aged adults and the nation's Social Security system, rates of repayment could be set to slightly more than replenish the funds (with interest) originally borrowed from the Social Security Trust Fund.

All generations would gain under such a system. Younger adults would enhance their earning power. The nation would benefit at once from better trained workers and parents in a stronger position to provide for children. And over time, the Social Security Trust Fund would grow, as loans were repaid and the national economy grows faster. The social and political logic of this way of reforming Social Security for the future makes even better sense than using projected federal tax surpluses to reduce the national debt and issue "IOUs" to the Social Security Trust Fund. The United States does not really need to reduce its national debt to zero; it can readily afford to run modest deficits in the future. If funds eventually needed for Social Security are used to boost the skills and earning power of younger families, this raises new revenues for the future and allows current payroll taxes to do "double duty," increasing the stake all Americans have in our shared system of social insurance.

Another possibility for building a cross-generational alliance involves extending social insurance to single working parents. When the Social Security system was first conceived during the New Deal, it was meant to address the chief "risks" of severe income loss that families might face over the course of a lifetime. Half a century later, however, important new risks are not addressed through our nation's social supports. Single-parent families, we have learned, are both more prevalent than ever before and highly pressured for time and money. These days many mothers (and quite a few fathers) end up combining family breadwinning with the nurture of children. Yet our legal system and social policies still treat single parenthood as if it were a freak occurrence. The burden is placed on the custodial parent, usually the mother. Especially if she is a woman with less than a college degree, a single working parent may simply not be able to earn a market income much above the poverty line. Furthermore, even middle-class single mothers often cannot work full-time while adequately caring for young children or managing the after-school activities of older offspring. Not just for economic reasons, but also because all of us want an orderly and participatory society—one where all single parents can supervise children and make it to soccer games—the nation as a whole has a very strong stake in improving the conditions faced by single-parent families.

Some years ago, policy experts proposed a cogent extension

of Social Security to make a big difference for single working parents at all income levels. The United States could institute a national system of Child Support Assurance.[7] Under this plan, either the Internal Revenue Service or the Social Security system would automatically deduct a set percentage of the wages of an absent parent (a percentage calibrated to the number of children requiring support) and deliver most of the money on a predictable and dignified monthly basis to the custodial parent. Because this would be an automatic step, caregiving parents would not be forced to go again and again to court or to a private collection agency to update awards and actually collect them. And noncustodial parents would face a more predictable and equitable system. Under a system of Child Support Assurance, America would be saying to all parents: you must contribute to the support of your children, and both caregiving and wage earning count. In return for contributing time, energy, and love on a daily basis, the custodial parent would receive some extra income beyond what she (or he) earns in the marketplace.

In an effective Child Support Assurance system, the burden of collection must be on the national government, which can use the payroll tax system and readily track absent parents across state lines using their Social Security numbers. What is more, the ideal Child Support Assurance system should include a fixed minimum benefit, set at about the level of a half-time minimum-wage job. Funded out of general federal revenues as well as from a very small increment to the payroll deductions collected from noncustodial parents, minimum payments would go to custodial parents in cases where the noncustodial parents cannot be found or earn insufficient income (for example, unemployed or imprisoned men). No caregiving parent could actually live on this minimum assured benefit; it would not be "welfare." But he or she could use the minimum benefit to enhance income from a job—or else cut back a bit on working hours in order to be at home with children at important times of the day, such as after school.

Child Support Assurance would make life more secure and

dignified for millions of American families, and thus for all of us indirectly. Both middle-class and low-income single mothers would be huge winners, giving millions more nonelderly Americans a stronger stake in social insurance. Yet this addition to Social Security could be created with little additional cost to the public fisc. True, a fraction of federal revenues would be committed to fund the minimum benefit at a reasonable level. But most of the revenues for child-support payments would come from automatic payroll deductions collected from noncustodial parents. The nation would gain a great deal for many vulnerable families, at very little new cost.

Some conservatives oppose national child-support collection as "more bureaucracy" and reject a guaranteed minimum benefit on the grounds that it might "reward" out-of-wedlock childbearing. These claims just do not bear scrutiny. National and automatic child-support collection would actually be much less complicated than the fragmented administrative and judicial system America now has. With or without a minimum floor under child-support benefits, moreover, the circumstances of single parents will remain economically and socially difficult. Few adults really want to raise children alone.

Conservatives have it backwards. Automatic child-support collections would probably discourage couples with children from breaking up or avoiding marriage. Certainly, a national system not easily evaded would make divorce or avoidance of marriage less appealing for fathers. For the past several decades, both conservative Republicans and new Democrats have focused sanctions to discourage out-of-wedlock childbearing on mothers—above all, on very poor mothers who might otherwise collect "welfare" benefits. This approach heaps opprobrium and material loss on top of the difficulties single mothers already face at home and in the market. Why not, instead, enhance predictable and dignified social support for working solo parents—while shifting the sanctions toward those noncustodial parents, usually fathers, who fail to meet their obligations?

151

There are, in short, some obvious ways to make Social Security, broadly conceived, do more than it has in the past for the vast majority of Americans—mitigating fiscal strains in the process. Extensions of our national systems of social security to fund training and help solo working parents would make economic and fiscal as well as social sense. Beyond the ideas discussed here, there may be other ways to extend Social Security as it is reformed. The policy specifics are less important than the principle: look for ways to build cross-generational and cross-class alliances through shared, rather than fragmented, systems of social support for all working families; provide new protections to citizens who are serving the nation as workers and parents; and find ways to generate additional revenues through economic growth and returns on investments, even as new protections are extended to younger Americans.

The Real Health Care Crisis

So far, I have focused on Social Security and related ways to enhance transfers through the payroll tax system. For Medicare (and Medicaid, which funds much care for the elderly as well as the poor), the situation is more complicated. Health care costs are not rising as fast as they were in the 1980s, but they are still going up. An aging population needs more, not less, medical care, even as expensive technological innovations create kinds of care that many people want. The United States really does face heightened health care costs in the early decades of the twenty-first century. The current, complex systems for financing Medicare—partly from payroll taxes, and partly from general federal revenues—are not going to be fully adequate without modifications in benefits and/or taxes.

Strains on our system of health insurance for the retired elderly coexist with the continuing inadequacy of our national system to cover health care costs for working-aged parents and their children. As we have seen, adults who work in low-wage or part-time jobs or self-employment, in particular, often go without any health insurance. And this situation is likely to get worse, not better, as employers switch to part-time jobs and cut back the coverage they are willing to offer to current employees and their family members. Another vulnerable group is employees in their late fifties and early sixties who retire or lose jobs before they have Medicare eligibility. Many employers will not cover early retirees; surviving spouses can be left uncovered; and older workers who lose jobs often cannot find new ones with full health insurance coverage.

During early 1998, the Clinton administration proposed extending Medicare eligibility to older men and women who lose jobs or retire without coverage, allowing them to buy into the existing system at a rate less than private insurance would cost, but enough to cover the additional costs to Medicare. This is a very good proposal, which extends Medicare into the pre-sixty-five-year-old population. Ideally, tax-financed subsidies should be offered to allow either less-privileged citizens or employers to buy into a steadily expanded Medicare system. Over time, many employers now struggling with the cost and administrative difficulties of health insurance might take up this option—and the existence of such a possibility for "buying into Medicare" could make it easier to require *all* employers to contribute to health insurance coverage for both full- and part-time employees.

Suggestions for extending rather than dismantling Medicare may sound unrealistic in a climate of expert opinion that seems, increasingly, to be calling for abandonment of Medicare's guarantees in favor of subsidies to privately funded "managed care" schemes. But the American citizenry may not buy the pundits' proposals as policy push comes to political shove in 1999 and 2000. Americans of all ages are worried about the steady march of managed care plans, and they may not take readily to the idea of subjecting the elderly to travails about care and insurance coverage that the young already know all too well.

Employers have shifted most covered employees into managed care systems, aspiring to save money on health care, yet managed care plans often cannot cut costs much, unless they restrict options for doctors and patients. Such steps are bound to be controversial in a society with an aging population and high expectations about health care. We already see cascading demands to regulate managed care systems, to enhance "choices" for patients and the clinical freedom of doctors. As new regulations are put in place, managed care plans will have trouble saving money; and many will abandon sick or vulnerable patient populations, as they already are doing.

"Reforms" of Medicare—including the expansion of managed care forms of delivery under careful federal regulatory oversight—ought to be devised in the context of steps to address overall shortfalls in American health care delivery and financing. Aiming to shrink government, conservatives criticize only the problems and shortcomings of governmentally financed health care. But Americans who care about shared provision and a decent society need to resist such cutbacks in the tax-supported financing of health care for large groups of Americans. Employer-funded health care is in crisis, too, as coverage shrinks and workers are forced to pay higher amounts for spottier services. Employment-based health insurance has never been the best way to include all Americans. Over time, a reformed and expanded system of "Medicare for all" may end up looking better and better to a majority of Americans—and not just for the elderly.

Support for All Working Families

So far, I have focused on America's inherited national systems of social insurance, suggesting ways to build new cross-generational linkages as social supports largely for the retired elderly are modified for the future. But "Saving Social Security and Medicare," no matter how creatively done, will not suffice to fill the missing middle of American social policy. Now should be a propitious moment to move on to new frontiers. Not only has the budgetary future brightened; for better as well as worse, "welfare" as we knew it prior to 1996 has been transformed. Major policy wars of the last generation can be declared over. With old battles behind us, we Americans can replace welfare assistance targeted on just a fraction of the very poor with enhanced social supports for all working families.

Many new supports must be devised and directed at the level of local communities, above all in conjunction with schools, churches, and community centers where parents and children routinely congregate. Beyond these, however, there must be new national initiatives, because only the federal government can enforce new rules for the market economy.

One of the greatest social scandals in late-twentieth-century America is the fate of men and women, including millions of fathers and mothers, who work daily and weekly at poorly paid full- and part-time jobs, but get such paltry wages that they find it virtually impossible to sustain families. The same workers often do not enjoy other benefits vital for families as well as individual workers—such as health insurance, employer contributions to pensions, and the right to take paid time off from work during family emergencies. Together, Americans can redress such injustices.

To their credit, the first and second Clinton administrations and Democrats in Congress have made some difference for low-income Americans. As part of the 1993 Budget Agreement proposed by President Clinton—and supported *only* by Democrats—the Earned Income Tax Credit (EITC) for low-wage working families was significantly increased to a level that helps lift many families with full-time workers above the poverty line. In 1996, too, Democrats successfully championed the first increase in the U.S. minimum wage enacted in many years. At that point, the real value of the U.S. minimum wage was the lowest it had been in some forty years.

More can and should be done along these lines in the near future. The minimum wage has still lost much of its real value in recent decades; if it were still at the same, inflation-adjusted level as it was in the 1970s, it would now be more than $6.30 an

155

hour, well above the level of $5.15 an hour legislated in 1996 to go into effect in 1997.[8] Americans concerned with social equity and family well-being should push for repeated increases in the minimum wage. Next time, it might be possible to pass a minimum-wage hike partially requiring employer contributions to health insurance and partially devoted to boosting take-home pay. Public support for raising the minimum wage, and general public support for the idea of asking all employers to contribute to health care, could be mobilized to move forward on two vital fronts for American working families. Although employer-financed health insurance is *not* the best option for America's long run, the sooner all employers have to pitch in, the easier it will become to move to a more unified system.

Enhanced social benefits available to both middle- and low-income workers are crucial for building a family-friendly America. Along with universal health insurance coverage, two other priorities are universal access to paid family leaves and affordable child care for working parents. The moral argument for these steps is clear-cut. Working mothers and fathers contribute to national well-being, not only as wage earners and taxpayers but also by bringing up children. They and their offspring deserve material support from the broader community to help meet today's challenges of combining work and family duties. Health care for all family members, time for family needs, and good child-care choices are all acutely needed by working families. Good policies can be designed to express broadly shared American values and promote solidarity across income levels and between single-parent and two-parent working families.

To help all American employees spend time with newborns and respond to emergencies in the care of young and old dependents, the 1993 Family and Medical Leave Act offers a starting place. But the "right" to take time off without losing one's job needs to be made a practicable option for all workers—and extended to all employees no matter what the size of the firm. Rights that apply disproportionately to privileged employees are not sufficient—certainly not the place to stop on the road to a family-friendly America. Realistically, making family leave a true right for American workers requires money. A combination of employer contributions and general tax revenues should be marshaled to cover the cost of *paid* family leaves. This could be done on a sliding scale for employers and employees alike: Smaller employers could receive more generous tax subsidies to cover family leaves; and the replacement of employee wages could be calibrated to give more to workers who earn modest wages and less (but still some) to the highest salaried employees who go on leave.

Family-friendly reforms should place a priority on ensuring supports for part-time as well as full-time (or overtime) workers. If part-time jobs had to include partial contributions to health insurance and pension benefits, employers would have less incentive to divide their workforces between full-time workers pressed to put in overtime and part-timers who go without benefits. That would help to ensure enough full-time jobs for all Americans who want to work. But at the same time, part-time jobs with pro-rated social benefits would help many single working parents, and would be a boon to married workers like Craig and Susan Miller, who try to sustain themselves and their children through a combination of various part-time jobs.

As more mothers engage in paid employment, long-term access to child care is a necessity for many solo-parent and two-worker-parent households. The need for solutions outside of family homes will become greater as women participate more and more fully in the labor force and stay-at-home grandmothers fade from the scene. Yet, today, quality child-care options are often not available; and families who take home low or modest wages find the cost of even mediocre child care prohibitive. As economist Barbara Bergmann has spelled out in detail, a national system of subsidized child care for all working parents who need it, while costly, would be a very effective antipoverty measure.[9] Such a system would also be a good investment in family well-being and early childhood education, with obvious payoffs for economic growth in the future.

Policy makers can get locked in battles over whether to provide child-care subsidies to institutions or to individual families. But it seems clear that both are needed. Subsidies to institutions—which should be made available to religious providers as well as others—are useful for increasing the availability of well-run and properly regulated facilities. And subsidies to families, perhaps channeled through tax credits that are refundable and thus available to low-wage workers, allow parents to choose and pay for appropriate care. Tax credits could be graduated, to deliver more help to less-well-off families; and parents could have freedom to choose among a variety of kinds of care meeting reasonable standards. In fact, tax subsidies should be structured to allow parents to choose time off work instead of, or in partial combination with, day-care centers or paid in-home caregivers.

Regulations and social benefits along the lines I have just covered will, of course, provoke strong opposition from conservatives—who claim that any "interference" with "free markets" is bad for economic growth. But a strong case can be made that exactly the opposite is true: capitalism works best when wise regulations and public expenditures buffer its rough edges. This is above all true when it comes to providing for family well-being. No economy, capitalist or otherwise, can long flourish if families cannot do their job of caring for the vulnerable and raising the young. Our nation's growing market economy is the underpinning of a decent life for most individuals and families, and we can be happy and proud that the economy has done so well in the 1990s. But it is a myth that vibrant market capitalism and adequate social supports for working families cannot go hand in hand. They can. In fact, America's economy will likely flourish in the new century only if we find optimal ways to spread the wealth and allow all families to raise healthy, well-educated, and well-supervised children. For those are tomorrow's workers, consumers, and citizens.

United States enterprises have done much to boost productivity and adjust to more competitive international markets. But competitive markets and agile enterprises do not automatically take account of the needs of families and communities. Public regulations are always needed to channel market forces in socially beneficial ways.[10] But America's economic regulations are outdated as well as incomplete. Indeed, they are so outdated that they often undermine market efficiency as such. Workers who have some security in their personal economic status and in their family lives tend to be more willing to adapt to changes on the job, and more willing to move from job to job to maximize productivity and career prospects.

As I have already noted, some U.S. market regulations, such as the minimum wage, have not kept up with inflation, so they provide much too little buffer for the lowest wage workers. Others, such as our rules about employer contributions to social benefits, have never been made complete enough to protect all employees, including part-timers and lower wage workers. And still other regulations—such as our rules about overtime work and work in the home—were devised with an earlier kind of economy and now-defunct family structures in mind.

Today we no longer have an economy centered around the father-breadwinner who goes off to work at a full-time (or more), well-paid, lifetime job, leaving behind a mother to care for the home and family. Instead, single-parent or two-worker families are prevalent. And part-time jobs, or combinations of them, are often the jobs available—and, at times, desired by working parents. Employees may need to change jobs, or at least skills, several times during their work careers. Employers want flexible and adaptable skilled employees. Computers make work at home possible for many.

Some enterprises are already adapting to all of these changes—but our public rules of the game for the economy do not usually ensure that adaptations will be fair to less-privileged employees, or take adequate account of social and family needs. Better pub-

159

lic policies—including health care and child care available to all citizens, and rules that part-time jobs should carry at least pro-rated benefits—would actually make the economy more efficient for employers as well as more equitable for employees at all wage levels. Working parents, above all, have a stake in such reforms, because they do not have the flexibility that other adults may have to switch jobs or scrimp on services such as health care.

Adjusting the employment system to new family realities should be America's top social priority, especially given welfare reforms that are pushing millions more single mothers into the low-wage paid-labor force. In a period of national economic growth, and at a time when all adults and parents are asked to make their way through paid employment, we in America should be asking: What kinds of employment conditions and public supports are needed to make it possible for all working parents to do their dual job? We should take strong steps to make sure that not just the highest paid employees, but all workers, can sustain families while working.

A Nation of Contributors

Ultimately, we should pursue a robust ideal. Because parents need time as well as money, we as a nation should work toward the norm of a thirty-five-hour workweek—with pay and benefits remaining at least at the level they were before the reduction in hours. However, this goal should not become a priority until after incomes and benefits are bolstered for low-wage working families. Work needs to pay, and be feasible in combination with single or dual parenthood, before we talk about a reduced national workweek. Otherwise, weekly reductions might simply redound to the benefit of skilled higher wage employees, leaving low-wage workers and their families in more desperate straits than ever.

This conclusion follows from the norms that have underpinned successful social policy making throughout American history. As I have argued, Americans favor broad social programs that reward individuals for "contributions" to the community. Contributions have been variously defined, of course, to include military service and motherhood as well as wage work. But at the turn of the twenty-first century, participation in the wage-employment system is universally understood as desirable for all adults, men and women, mothers and fathers alike. We can do much to reinforce social understanding that parental work is also valuable for the community. But Americans cannot be convinced that parental work apart from at least part-time waged employment is socially honorable. Americans should strengthen and buffer the nexus of wage work and family. In our time, revitalizing the long tradition of U.S. social policy making that says citizens are worthy of social benefits in return for contributions to the community means focusing our efforts on the contributions and well-being of worker-parents, who are also expected to be involved citizens.

Many progressives who read this book will worry about my repeated stress on "family" well-being, and my claim that children ideally need the support of two married parents. In recent decades, many progressives have been unwilling to highlight family needs or champion two-parent households for fear of appearing to ostracize single mothers. But surely Americans of all political persuasions can acknowledge that children do best in two-parent families supported by the nation and local communities, without denying that single-parent families also deserve our support. Public policies can support married parenthood, and at the same time channel assistance to the many divorced and single parents who are doing the best they can. In most areas of social policy, dual-worker families with children and solo-parent families actually have convergent interests; and their children are inevitably raised together. Finding and meeting shared (or overlapping) family needs should be a progressive priority, and this approach is certainly smart progressive politics.[11]

Taken together, the undertakings I have suggested would amount to a revitalization and extension of broad, shared social supports. Instead of allowing conservatives to dismantle shared social protections for the elderly in the name of righting the balance for working-aged adults and their children, America can extend social supports to include younger families—especially the families of modest means who are currently left beyond the reach of many publicly funded or employment-linked benefits.

To take this course it will be necessary to revalue national government as an instrument for addressing broadly shared needs in the name of democratically shared values. Tax revenues will be needed—although the burden becomes lighter as the economy grows and federal indebtedness shrinks. Modest reforms of U.S. taxes could help to generate resources for a more just society. As the biggest "winners" in the economy since the 1970s, the top third or so of income earners could easily pay proportionately more income tax. And Congress could lift the "cap" on payroll taxes for Social Security and Medicare, so that employees at all income levels pay a full share. Other changes might be more fundamental, but nevertheless salutary. The United States could shift some of its tax burden away from payroll taxes that fall heavily on young working families by creating new consumption levies designed to raise revenue from expenditures on items that are beyond basic necessities for families.

Many voices have argued that it may be time to overhaul the national tax system. Advocates across the partisan spectrum have a point when they say America should devise a simpler system that rewards productive investments and encourages public and private savings. Fundamental reforms may well be in order. But they should not be conceived as "revenue-neutral" changes; still less as yet another round of tax cuts for the privileged. Rather, we should devise a fair and economically wise tax system that raises enhanced revenues to sustain adequate social supports for the future. All working families should contribute according to their means; and all should be able to count on dignified support from the larger community.

WILL AMERICANS SUPPORT IT?

The call to reconfigure social supports to build a family-friendly America amounts to a moral vision, not just a laundry list of legislative prescriptions. This runs against the grain of politics today, because our national conversations seem increasingly dominated by policy wonks and economists mired in technical details, or by media people focusing on short-term personal maneuvers and scandals. However, from the 1960s through the 1980s, conservatives in America showed that a politics of broad social mobilization around clearly articulated values, not just narrow policy prescriptions, could move the center of national debate and reshape the landscape of politics. Now it is time for Americans who believe government has a pivotal role to play in building a just society to undertake a similarly bold and visionary strategy.

A family-oriented populism focused especially on working parents can revitalize the tradition of successful social policy making in American democracy—generating civic dividends in the process. Americans believe in linking national supports to important individual contributions to community well-being. Mobilizing government to work with nongovernmental institutions to better support parents is an endeavor very much within this vital tradition.

Pursuit of supports for working families can strengthen Americans' sense of community—not just in particular localities, but also across lines of class and race. To transcend the racial conflicts that have so divided and weakened our nation since the 1960s, supporters of social provision can combine continuing efforts to carve out new opportunities for African Americans with pursuit of social programs relevant to Americans of all ethnic and racial groups. A family-oriented strategy does both of these things. Supports for working families are especially vital for African Americans, who often find themselves in a tighter economic and family squeeze than other Americans. Yet Americans of all ethnic and racial groups also need economic redress and social support. Shared programs will do the most for the severely disadvantaged, while significantly helping middle-class Americans at the same time.[12]

A family-oriented politics does not depend on everyone being a parent or part of "the same kind of family." The issue is not sheer numbers of potential voters counted up as isolated individuals. Not every American adult is a parent; in fact there are more U.S. adults living alone and proportionately fewer families with children than ever before. But sheer demography has never been destiny for social policy in the United States. Perceived contributions to the community matter more, as do possibilities for cross-class ties. Issues of parental responsibility and social support for parents can become a sympathetic focus for almost all citizens.

Consider retirees, for example. They may not be active parents right now; but most are grandparents who care about their children and grandchildren. Elders also understand the nation's and their own stake in productive workers. It is an odd feature of U.S. politics today that so many pundits are declaring "generational warfare" just as the country faces the prospect of more elders but fewer dependent children per adult worker. If work and family can be made to mesh more smoothly—helping adults to become optimally productive even as they are engaged and effective parents—then retirees, working-aged adults, and children will all do well together. An aging society is not at all a zero-sum game.

Because support for families and working parents holds out the prospect of broad electoral appeal and alliance building, this strategy may hold the key to revitalizing and broadening a progressive Democratic Party. Women voters often favor politicians, mostly Democrats, who favor social supports for families. Yet such measures need not alienate most men, because they include steps to improve wage and benefit conditions vital to husbands and fathers. A vision built around the well-being of families is also likely to prove very appealing to Hispanic voters, who represent a vital new voting bloc for Democrats. This approach should help to mobilize cross-racial support in the South as well.

A morally grounded appeal to shared concerns does better in American politics than any explicit call for class-based mobilization. The needs of less-privileged Americans must be made central to reconfigured social supports, but I disagree with some on the left who are calling for an overtly "working class"–oriented populism. It is not just that there are too few unionized employees in late-twentieth-century America. There certainly *are* too few—and unions need to be supported and strengthened by everyone who professes concern for a vital civil society. But even if unions were to regain the economic and electoral leverage they enjoyed back in the 1950s—when more than a third of U.S. workers were unionized, as opposed to less than a seventh now—explicitly class-oriented politics would not suffice to remake American social provision. A popular politics featuring a vision of solidarity and security for all families can resonate with a revitalized labor movement and at the same time facilitate broader coalitions and ties between middle-class and downscale Americans. This kind of politics can also engage the energies of religious leaders and congregations, who can do more than any other force in American civic life to articulate why, as the U.S. Catholic Bishops so eloquently put it, "[a]ll economic life should be judged by moral principles. Economic choices and institutions must be judged by how they protect or undermine the life and dignity of the human person, support the family, and serve the common good."[13]

ORGANIZING FOR DEMOCRATIC CHANGE

American social politics will not change simply because people write books. And it is equally clear that politics-as-usual is unlikely to allow working families much leverage in public policy making. Sure, political consultants may advise candidates to talk about "American families" during campaigns or in televised speeches. We can expect a lot of such talk during the run-up to the presidential contests for 2000. But when it comes to the legislative nitty-gritty, close attention is likely to be paid to what the best organized and monied interests are saying, or to what the most prominent "experts" propose. Being realistic about getting legislation through Congress will, in the minds of many, dictate sacrificing the interests and values of ordinary working families— especially when budgets remain tight and it is taken for granted that taxes must be cut or left unchanged.

A new vision can help inspire the popular support to change this status quo. But people must also be *organized*—reconnected to ongoing civic and party activities as Margaret Weir and Marshall Ganz have explained in their brilliant essay "Reconnecting People and Politics."[14] At least two processes of popular mobilization and reorganization of politics need to proceed hand in hand, if American democracy is to reach for the missing middle. One process is frankly partisan, rebuilding the Democratic Party from the bottom up. The other departure should be transpartisan, a process of connecting centers of family activity across communities and states into a nationwide civic association of, by, and for the vast majority of America's families.

The Democratic Party for Real

At one time, for better and worse, the Democratic Party was grounded in a series of local and state "political machines." There were disadvantages and social inequities in this situation. Party platforms and nominations tended to be brokered in those famous smoke-filled rooms, to which only loyal cadres were admitted. In most communities, African Americans and other minorities either had no place in the party bargains, or else were expected to take minor rewards in return for faithfully turning out to vote. Women were expected to stuff envelopes and provide a symbolic presence, not to shape insider bargains.

But at least there was a "there" in the old-time Democratic

Party. There were people and headquarters you could go to, to ask for something, to join in discussions, or to work on getting out the vote. There were activists who went out and contacted fellow citizens and asked them to vote or volunteer. Today the "Democratic Party" amounts to little more than a series of mass mailings and centers for collecting checks. Every month or so, I get a letter from some Democratic Party office: a long canned statement, hopelessly bland, accompanied by a fake questionnaire, a tear-out wallet "membership card," and—of course, the real point—a return card and envelope for me to use to send a big check. The party tells me, in the form letter, that it wants my opinions. But it really just wants my money so it can pay pollsters and consultants. In turn, party officials, or consultants hired by the party, tell individual candidates how to word their media messages and speeches to attract particular sets of swing voters—and after the election how to phrase their messages explaining votes or "policy achievements." The consultants pretty much *are* the Democratic Party. In most communities and states, there are few opportunities for regular Democrats to talk with one another, or to talk back to the consultants and candidates. The people who talk to one another are the consultants.

There are organized groups surrounding the Democratic Party and some, like the revitalized AFL-CIO under John Sweeney, have significant popular roots. So do groups in the environmental movement and the National Organization for Women, which includes local chapters. But most Democratic-leaning advocacy groups are themselves little more than mass mailing and check collecting operations. Centered in New York or Washington, staff professionals decide what issues to raise with government and political candidates. In such advocacy groups, as in today's political parties, there is little opportunity for regularly meeting groups of citizens to take part in two-way conversations.

A new network of progressive Democratic groups needs to be knit together—a real counterweight to the Democratic Leadership Council—but not just centered in Washington, D.C. Progressive Democrats certainly need national centers of publication, communication, research, and advocacy. To a considerable degree these already exist: *The American Prospect* and *The Washington Monthly* are Democratic-leaning magazines. The Economic Policy Institute, the Institute for Women's Policy Research, and the Center on Budget and Policy Priorities are Democratic-leaning research centers of the highest order. And the Campaign for America's Future is an energetic populist Democratic advocacy group. In addition to these central institutions, though, progressive Democrats should foster a self-conscious network of actual groups, where people who consider themselves Democrats or party sympathizers get together regularly for fun and discussion. Over time, such groups can help to shape platforms, select and support candidates, and highlight issues in the larger community.

What is more—and this is the tricky part—any such network of progressive Democrats needs to be grounded in, and in regular touch with, ongoing social settings where individuals and families of modest means go about daily activities. Otherwise, groups could just become sets of issue activists. A way needs to be found to deepen activism within the Democratic Party, while keeping in touch with cultural common sense and the economic experiences of less-privileged Americans.

There is nothing radical about this suggestion, really. If a revitalized, majority Democratic Party were to lead the way toward a new partnership with working families, the result would almost surely be to recapture—and extend—the best traditions of U.S. social policy making, stretching all the way back into the nineteenth century. As we have learned, again and again—and starting long before Franklin Roosevelt's New Deal—successful U.S. social policies have furthered economic security and opportunity for many American families, while simultaneously expressing and reinforcing mainstream moral values about family integrity, individual responsibility, and the mutual obligations of individuals and the national community. Democrats who decide to champion family security do not need to imitate any foreign models, or take any unprecedented leaps into an unhinged future. They do not even have to cling to the New Deal as the sole progressive precedent. They only need to discover fresh ways to involve and keep in touch with the outlooks of ordinary voters, so that Democrats can champion and build majority support for a new version of American social provision at its best.

Families Associated

Progressive Democrats should mobilize and organize, but the middle cannot be revitalized through partisan activation alone. There must also be a renewal of associational activities centered in membership groups of actual working parents who get together regularly to deal with family issues. Throughout most of American history until the 1970s, huge, vital voluntary associations linked membership lodges or clubs in thousands of local communities into federated organizations that had real presence, and recurrent meetings, in each state and at the national level.[15] The Patrons of Husbandry, or Grange, did this for millions of American farm families. Fraternal groups and veterans' associations and their ladies' auxiliaries did this for most working- and middle-class American men and their wives. Similar local and translocal ties developed among women involved in church-related associations, the Woman's Christian Temperance Union, the National Congress of Mothers (which became the National Congress of Parents and Teachers, or PTA, in 1924), and the General Federation of Women's Clubs. Some such popularly rooted voluntary associations still exist in the United States. But they have almost all lost much of their membership and clout since the 1960s. Today's biggest association is the American Association of Retired Persons, which largely recruits and communicates with members through the mail.

Various people these days are thinking of trying to build a nationwide movement or association of parents. The National Parenting Association, for instance, is talking about establishing an "AARP for parents."[16] A new association may make sense, but

169

the AARP may not be an ideal model. Parents are busy people, and none more so than working moms and dads in single-parent or two-worker families. So to engage them means to build from occasions, places, and networks in which they are already involved with one another—especially because of the need to do things with and for their children. Ways should be found to build—and extensively interconnect—actual groups of parents involved with day-care centers, church groups, after-school activities, sports activities, and support groups for parents of young children and people caring for the frail elderly. A new family movement in America needs newsletters, meetings, a real identity—complete with symbols and logos—as well as discounts and information of the sort that the AARP provides. But it would be better to build from the ground up and rely much more than does the AARP on membership participation and dues. A new family movement needs to build on connections and institutions that are already there—so that it can be rooted in actual relationships among ordinary citizens. Parent-members must actually control the movement.

Given the way organization building now happens in America, it will be challenging to create a broad movement rather than many narrow cause or identity organizations. We need a Movement for America's Families, not an organization of Hispanic families plus an organization of elder caregivers, plus an organization of parents of difficult teenagers, etc. Around a central association there can and should be more specific efforts, but the sum must be bigger and more central than the parts.

The Way Forward

Americans who care about recentering our civic and political life must, in short, pursue strategies that look further ahead than the usual Washington time horizon of the day after tomorrow. With public intellectuals self-consciously taking bolder stands than most elected politicians can be expected to embrace at any given moment, supporters of a more equitable society and stronger social supports for families must frankly proclaim their moral vision, linking it to specific proposals. They must organize inside and outside the electoral system, and push politicians and other institutional leaders toward a bolder stand on behalf of *all* working parents and their children, even as broad swatches of Americans are brought together for action and discussion about the needs of communities and families.

The pursuit of social supports for America's families—with a special emphasis on moral and material sustenance for working parents—holds great democratic promise. Efforts to organize on behalf of this vision, as well as debates about it, will be healthy for America—even if a lot of legislation cannot be "moved" in Congress tomorrow. Security and opportunity for all families, honor and support for all parents—these are goals that can transform American civic life and reshape national social supports to include everyone, working parents and children along with our grandparents. Pursuit of family-friendly institutions and public policies can unite millions of Americans in support of shared undertakings to address the real social challenges of our time. We can, in short, shape a democracy that *will* make life better for—and in partnership with—the Annemarie McAndrews and the Craig and Susan Millers of our time.

NOTES

CHAPTER ONE

1. "Announcement Speech," Old State House, Little Rock, Arkansas, October 2, 1991, reprinted in Governor Bill Clinton and Senator Al Gore, *Putting People First: How We Can All Change America* (New York: Times Books, 1992), p. 196.
2. Clinton and Gore, *Putting People First*, pp. 8, 5, 14.
3. Ibid., pp. 8–9.
4. Ibid., p. 6.
5. Quotes come from "The Text of the President's State of the Union Address to Congress," *New York Times*, January 20, 1999, pp. A22–23.
6. For an assessment of the 1990s expansion, see Louis Uchitelle, "Muscleman, Or 98-Pound Weakling? Taking the Measure of an 8-Year Economic Expansion," *New York Times*, October 18, 1998, section 3, pp. 1, 11.
7. Lester C. Thurow, "The Boom That Wasn't," *New York Times*, January 18, 1999, p. A19. For additional, in-depth perspectives, differing in certain technical respects but arriving at many similar conclusions, about wage and income trends, see: Lawrence Mishel, Jared Bernstein, and John Schmitt, *The State of Working America, 1998–99* (Ithaca, NY: Cornell University Press); and David T. Ellwood, "Winners and Losers in America: Taking the Measure of the New Economic Realities," John F. Kennedy School of Government, Harvard University, 1998, forthcoming in a book (as yet untitled) to be published by the Russell Sage Foundation, New York City.
8. John E. Schwarz, "The Hidden Side of the Clinton Economy," *The Atlantic Monthly* 282(4) (October 1998), p. 21.
9. See Tables 3.15 and 3.16 in Mishel, Bernstein, and Schmitt, *State of Working America, 1998–99*, pp. 146–47.

10. Sue Shellenbarger, "Family Leave Is Law, but Climate Is Poor for Actually Taking It," *Wall Street Journal*, October 30, 1996, p. B1. For a discussion of eligibility restrictions and practical limits on workers choosing to take unpaid leaves, see Commission on Family and Medical Leave, *A Workable Balance: Report to Congress on Family and Medical Leave Policies* (Washington, DC: U.S. Department of Labor, Women's Bureau, 1996).

11. See U.S. Census Bureau, "Health Insurance Coverage: 1997," in the March 1998 *Current Population Survey*.

12. U.S. Bureau of the Census, "The Haves and the Have-Nots," in *Current Population Reports*, Series P60–202 (September 1998).

13. I tell this story in Theda Skocpol, *Boomerang: Health Care Reform and the Turn Against Government* (New York: W. W. Norton, 1997).

14. Polling results showing popular willingness to pay for inclusive social programs appear again and again. Instances of majority willingness to contribute is, for example, documented in Robert J. Blendon, Mollyann Brodie, and John M. Benson, "What Happened to Americans' Support of the Clinton Plan," *Health Affairs 14*(2) (Summer 1995), pp. 15–17; in Stanley B. Greenberg's post-election survey for the Campaign for America's Future, "The Popular Mandate of 1996" (Washington, DC: Greenberg Research, 1996); and in the W. K. Kellogg Foundation, "Devolution Survey on Healthcare and Welfare Reform Issues," released January 13, 1999, Table 17. I obtained data from this survey at the website <http://www.wkkf.org>.

15. Sylvia Ann Hewlett and Cornel West, *The War Against Parents: What We Can Do for America's Beleaguered Moms and Dads* (Boston, MA: Houghton Mifflin, 1998), p. 261. See also the Kellogg Foundation's "Devolution Survey," Table 3, where 57 percent of respondents to a national poll cited perceptions that "their involvement makes no difference" or "they don't know how to become involved" as reasons why "more people aren't involved in changing/supporting public policy."

16. Opinions of parents themselves, as expressed in a poll sponsored by the National Parenting Association, are summarized in Hewlett and West, *War Against Parents*, Appendix A.

17. See Kellogg Foundation, "Devolution Survey."

18. See the typical full-page Concord Coalition advertisement, headlined "America's Real Deficit Problem is Still Out There—and Now is the Time to Do Something About It," *New York Times*, July 13, 1997, p. 21. A fuller version of the Concord Coalition argument appears in Peter G. Peterson, *Facing Up: How to Rescue the Economy from Crushing Debt and Restore the American Dream* (New York: Simon and Schuster, 1993), and Peter G. Peterson, *Will America Grow Up Before It Grows Old?* (New York: Random House, 1996).

19. Sheldon Danziger and Peter Gottschalk, *America Unequal* (Cambridge, MA: Harvard University Press, 1995); and Bureau of the Census, *Current Population Survey* (Washington, DC: Government Printing Office, 1997). For more recent analyses, see the citations in note 7 above.

20. James Garbarino, *Raising Children in a Socially Toxic Environment* (San Francisco, CA: Jossey-Bass, 1995).

21. The phrase comes from the title of John J. Sweeney, *America Needs a Raise: Fighting for Economic Security and Social Justice* (Boston, MA: Houghton Mifflin, 1996).

22. For one striking statement along these lines, see Ben J. Wattenberg, *Values Matter Most* (New York: Free Press, 1995). See also the Democratic Leadership Council's magazine, *The New Democrat*.

23. For example, Barbara Dafoe Whitehead, *The Divorce Culture* (New York: Knopf, 1996).

24. Newt Gingrich, *Window of Opportunity: A Blueprint for the Future* (New York: Tom Doherty Associates and St. Martin's Press, 1984); and Newt Gingrich, *To Renew America* (New York: HarperCollins, 1995).

25. See, for example, the framing of the issues in Children's Defense Fund, *Wasting America's Future* (Boston, MA: Beacon Press, 1994).

26. For such opinion results, see Hewlett and West, *War Against Parents*, Appendix A; and the Kellogg Foundation, "Devolution Survey," especially Tables 15 and 32.

27. Robert Pear, "New Effort Aims to Enroll Children in Insurance Plans," *New York Times*, February 23, 1999, p. A11. This article chronicles earlier failed Clinton administration "campaigns" to sign up children alone for a bewildering variety of state-level insurance assistance plans.

28. For examples, see Marvin Olasky, *The Tragedy of American Compassion* (Wheaton, IL: Crossway Books, 1992); and Michael S. Joyce and William A. Schambra, "A New Civic Life," pp. 11–29 in *To Empower People: From State to Civil Society*, second edition, edited by Michael Novak (Washington, DC: AEI Press, 1996).

CHAPTER TWO

1. See Sylvia Ann Hewlett and Cornel West, *The War Against Parents: What We Can Do for America's Beleaguered Moms and Dads* (Boston, MA: Houghton Mifflin, 1998), p. 266; and Paul Pierson, "The Deficit and the Politics of Domestic Reform," pp. 126–78 in *The Social Divide: Political Parties and the Future of Activist Government*, edited by Margaret Weir (Washington, DC: Brookings Institution Press, and New York: Russell Sage Foundation, 1998).

2. Paul Pierson and Miriam Smith, "Retrenchment and Generational Conflict: The Shifting Political Fortunes of Programs for the Elderly," in *Economic Security, Intergenerational Justice, and the North American*

Elderly (Washington, DC: The Urban Institute Press, 1994); Jill Quadagno, "Generational Equity and the Politics of the Welfare State," *Politics and Society 17*(3) (1989), pp. 353–76; and Paul Adams and Gary L. Dominick, "The Old, the Young, and the Welfare State," *Generations 19*(3) (Fall 1995), pp. 38–42.

3. *Aging America: Trends and Projections*, 1991 edition (Washington, DC: U.S. Department of Health and Human Services, 1991), p. 251, Chart 9-1.

4. Richard B. Freeman, editor, *Working Under Different Rules* (New York: Russell Sage Foundation, 1994); and Timothy Smeeding, "American Income Inequality in Cross-National Perspective" (Syracuse University, May 1997).

5. Ira Katznelson and Margaret Weir, *Schooling for All: Class, Race, and the Decline of the Democratic Ideal* (New York: Basic Books, 1985), Chapter 2; and Arnold J. Heidenheimer, "Education and Social Security Entitlements in Europe and America," pp. 269–304 in *The Development of Welfare States in Europe and America*, edited by Peter Flora and Arnold J. Heidenheimer (New Brunswick, NJ: Transaction Books, 1981).

6. Theda Skocpol, *Protecting Soldiers and Mothers: The Political Origins of Social Policy in the United States* (Cambridge, MA: The Belknap Press of Harvard University Press, 1992), pp. 129–35.

7. Ibid., Chapters 7 and 8.

8. Ibid., Chapter 9; and Molly Ladd-Taylor, *Raising a Baby the Government Way: Mothers' Letters to the Children's Bureau, 1915-1932* (New Brunswick, NJ: Rutgers University Press, 1986).

9. Martha Derthick, *Policymaking for Social Security* (Washington, DC: Brookings Institution Press, 1979).

10. Theodore R. Marmor, *The Politics of Medicare* (Chicago, IL: Aldine, 1970).

11. "The GI Bill's Lasting Legacy," special issue of the *Educational Record 75*(4) (Fall 1994); Theodore R. Mosch, *The G.I. Bill: A Breakthrough in Educational and Social Policy in the United States* (Hicksville, NY: Exposition Press, 1975); and Michael J. Bennett, *When Dreams Came True: The GI Bill and the Making of Modern America* (Washington, DC: Brassey's, 1996).

12. From Donald Bruce Johnson, *National Party Platforms*, volume 1, revised edition (Urbana, IL: University of Illinois Press, 1978), p. 82.

13. "Message to Congress on the Education of War Veterans," October 27, 1943, in *The Public Papers and Addresses of Franklin D. Roosevelt*, volume 12, *The Tide Turns: 1943*, compiled by Samuel I. Rosenman (New York: Russell and Russell, 1950; reissued 1969), pp. 450–51.

14. Mustafa Emirbayer, "The Shaping of a Virtuous Citizenry: Educational

Reform in Massachusetts, 1830–1860," *Studies in American Political Development* 6 (Fall 1992), pp. 391–419; and David Tyack and Elisabeth Hansot, *Managers of Virtue: Public School Leadership in America, 1820–1980* (New York: Basic Books, 1982), Part I.

15. Mrs. G. H. Robertson, "The State's Duty to Fatherless Children," *Child-Welfare Magazine* 6(5) (January 1912), pp. 156–57. For an overview of the arguments for mothers' pensions, see Skocpol, *Protecting Soldiers and Mothers*, Chapter 8.

16. See the data and discussion in Stanley B. Greenberg, "The Economy Project" (Washington, DC: Greenberg Research, January 16, 1996).

17. Skocpol, *Protecting Soldiers and Mothers*, p. 138.

18. Keith W. Olson, *The G.I. Bill, the Veterans, and the Colleges* (Lexington, KY: University Press of Kentucky, 1974), especially Chapters 3–6; Clark Kerr, "Expanding Access and Changing Missions: The Federal Role in U.S. Higher Education," *Educational Record* 75(4) (Fall 1994), pp. 27–31; and Michael J. Bennett, *When Dreams Came True: The GI Bill and the Making of Modern America* (Washington, DC: Brassey's, 1996).

19. The text of the enabling act appears in *First Annual Report of the Chief, Children's Bureau to the Secretary of Labor for the Year Ended June 30, 1913* (Washington, DC: Government Printing Office, 1914), p. 2.

20. Louis J. Covotsos, "Child Welfare and Social Progress: A History of the United States Children's Bureau, 1912–1935" (Ph.D. dissertation, University of Chicago, 1976), p. 123.

21. From a letter by Julia Lathrop to Bleeker Marquette, December 1, 1920, Children's Bureau Papers, Drawer 408, National Archives, Washington, DC, as quoted in Covotsos, "Child Welfare," p. 123.

22. On the initial exclusion of most African Americans and the later expansion of Social Security to include those who were employed, see Robert C. Lieberman, *Shifting the Color Line: Race and the American Welfare State* (Cambridge, MA: Harvard University Press, 1998).

23. Tyack and Hansot, *Managers of Virtue*, p. 17.

24. The overall story is told in detail in Skocpol, *Protecting Soldiers and Mothers*, Part III. For a statistical analysis, see Theda Skocpol, Christopher Howard, Susan Goodrich Lehmann, and Marjorie Abend-Wein, "Women's Associations and the Enactment of Mothers' Pensions in the United States," *American Political Science Review* 87(3) (September 1993), pp. 686–701.

25. On the WCTU, see Ruth Bordin, *Woman and Temperance: The Quest for Power and Liberty, 1873–1900* (New Brunswick, NJ: Rutgers University Press, 1990; orig. 1981); and Barbara Leslie Epstein, *The Politics of Domesticity: Women, Evangelism, and Temperance in Nineteenth-Century America* (Middletown, CT: Wesleyan University Press, 1981).

26. Karen J. Blair, *The Clubwoman as Feminist: True Womanhood Redefined, 1868–1914* (New York: Holmes and Meier, 1980); and Mary I. Wood, *The History of the General Federation of Women's Clubs for the First Twenty-Two Years of Its Organization* (New York: History Department, GFWC, 1912).

27. This statement was for some years part of the "Aims and Purposes of the National Congress of Mothers," as listed in a box in each issue of the organization's official magazine. See, for example, *Child-Welfare Magazine* 7(2) (October 1912), p. 61. For an official history of the National Congress (later the PTA), see *Golden Jubilee History, 1897–1947* (Chicago, IL: National Congress of Parents and Teachers, 1947). A good discussion of the evolution of the National Congress of Mothers into the PTA appears in Steven L. Schlossman, "Before Home Start: Notes toward a History of Parent Education in America," *Harvard Educational Review* 46(3) (August 1976), pp. 436–67. On the Congress's role in maternalist policy making, see Skocpol, *Protecting Soldiers and Mothers*, Part III; and Molly Ladd-Taylor, *Mother-Work: Women, Child Welfare, and the State, 1890–1930* (Urbana: University of Illinois Press, 1994).

28. Sadly, the remarkable alliance of female professional advocates and grassroots women's federations that achieved so many social policy milestones in the early 1900s ceased to be a major force after the mid-1920s. After American women won the right to vote with the passage of the Nineteenth Amendment in 1920, it only took a few years for politicians to realize that women would not vote together. Simultaneously, as government programs for mothers and children were established, there was a tendency for some of them to become bureaucratized and dominated by professionals. The leaders of women's voluntary federations were tempted to deal just with social service professionals and with Congress, without turning to grassroots mobilization as much as they had done back in the 1910s. During the 1920s conservatives opposed to social programs attacked the women's federations, accusing them of having "communist" tendencies because of their support for social programs. After the middle of the 1920s, the federations retreated from social and political activism. The National Congress of Mothers became like the present-day Parent-Teacher Association, devoting its energies to working with local school boards and no longer seeking to carry "mother-thought" into all spheres of life and legislation. Many of the groups making up the General Federation of Women's Clubs turned away from broad civic concerns toward purely literary and cultural activities. The grand era of married women's political activism in U.S. democracy came to an end, or at least a pause.

29. On the American Legion's membership, structure, and activities, see Richard Seelye Jones, *A History of the American Legion* (New York: Bobbs-Merrill, 1946); and William Pencak, *For God and Country: The American Legion, 1919–1941* (Boston, MA: Northeastern University Press, 1989).

30. The Legion's impact on the GI Bill and other World War II veterans' legislation is amply documented by Davis R. B. Ross, *Preparing for Ulysses: Politics and Veterans During World War II* (New York: Columbia University Press, 1969); and Bennett, *When Dreams Came True*, Chapter 3.

31. On the Townsend Movement and its impact, see Abraham Holtzman, *The Townsend Movement: A Political Study* (New York: Bookman, 1963); and Edwin Amenta, Bruce G. Carruthers, and Yvonne Zylan, "A Hero for the Aged? The Townsend Movement, the Political Mediation Model, and U.S. Old-Age Policy, 1934–1950," *American Journal of Sociology* 98(2) (September 1992), pp. 308–39.

32. See Skocpol, *Protecting Soldiers and Mothers*, pp. 107–30, and the references in note 30 above.

33. Skocpol, *Protecting Soldiers and Mothers*, pp. 491–512.

34. A classic presentation of this argument is Paul E. Peterson, *City Limits* (Chicago, IL: University of Chicago Press, 1981).

35. Although they may support income transfers to the young more readily than other Americans do, a majority of the elderly do *not* support increased spending on education. See Michael Ponza, Greg J. Duncan, Mary Corcoran, and Fred Groskind, "The Guns of Autumn? Age Differences in Support for Income Transfers to the Young and Old," *Public Opinion Quarterly* 52(4) (Winter 1988), pp. 441–66.

36. This overall point is brilliantly argued and thoroughly documented in Edwin Amenta, *Bold Relief: Institutional Politics and the Origins of Modern American Social Policy* (Princeton, NJ: Princeton University Press, 1998).

37. Richard Franklin Bensel, *Sectionalism and American Political Development, 1880–1980* (Madison, WI: University of Wisconsin Press, 1984), Chapter 3.

38. Heywood T. Sanders, "Paying for the 'Bloody Shirt': The Politics of Civil War Pensions," in *Political Benefits*, edited by Barry S. Rundquist (Lexington, MA: Lexington Books, D. C. Heath, 1980), pp. 150–54.

39. John F. Witte, *The Politics and Development of the Federal Income Tax* (Madison, WI: University of Wisconsin Press, 1985); and W. Elliot Brownlee, editor, *Funding the Modern American State, 1941–1995: The Rise and Fall of the Era of Easy Finance* (Washington, DC: Woodrow Wilson Center Press and Cambridge University Press, 1996).

40. Carolyn C. Jones, "Mass-Based Income Taxation: Creating a Taxpaying Culture, 1940–1952," pp. 107–47 in *Funding the Modern American State*, edited by W. Elliot Brownlee.

41. Edward D. Berkowitz, "The First Advisory Council and the 1939 Amendments," pp. 55–78 in *Social Security After Fifty: Successes and Failures*, edited by Edward Berkowitz (Westport, CT: Greenwood Press, 1987).

42. Derthick, *Policymaking for Social Security*, pp. 198–201; and Cheryl Zollars and Theda Skocpol, "Cultural Mythmaking as a Policy Tool: The Social Security Board and the Construction of a Social Citizenship of Self Interest," pp. 381–408 in "Political Culture and Political Structure: Theoretical and Empirical Studies," edited by Frederick D. Weil for *Research on Democracy and Society, volume 2* (Greenwich, CT: JAI Press, 1994).

43. Norman Furniss and Timothy Tilton, *The Case for the Welfare State* (Bloomington, IN: Indiana University Press, 1977).

44. Katherine S. Newman, *Declining Fortunes: The Withering of the American Dream* (New York: Basic Books, 1993).

45. Sheldon Danziger and Peter Gottschalk, *America Unequal* (Cambridge, MA: Harvard University Press; and New York: Russell Sage Foundation, 1995).

46. James T. Patterson, *America's Struggle Against Poverty, 1900–1980* (Cambridge, MA: Harvard University Press, 1981), Parts III and IV.

47. Quadagno, "Generational Equity," pp. 355–56.

48. Marian Wright Edelman, *Families in Peril: An Agenda for Social Change* (Cambridge, MA: Harvard University Press, 1987), p. ix.

49. David Alan Stockman, *The Triumph of Politics* (New York: Harper and Row, 1986).

50. Stuart Butler and Peter Germanis, "Achieving a Leninist Strategy," *Cato Journal 3* (Fall 1983), pp. 547–61. See also Thomas Conley Rollins, Jr., "The New Politics of Social Security" (Unpublished Senior Honors Essay, Harvard College, March 1998), Chapter 4.

51. Peter G. Peterson, *Facing Up: How to Rescue the Economy from Crushing Debt and Restore the American Dream* (New York: Simon and Schuster, 1993).

52. Marmor, *Politics of Medicare*.

53. Margaret Weir, *Politics and Jobs: The Boundaries of Employment Policy in the United States* (Princeton, NJ: Princeton University Press, 1992).

54. Patterson, *America's Struggle Against Poverty*, Chapters 10–11.

55. The story is well told in Thomas Byrne Edsall and Mary D. Edsall, *Chain Reaction: The Impact of Race, Rights, and Taxes on American Politics* (New York: W. W. Norton, 1991).

56. Kathryn Edin and Laura Lein, *Making Ends Meet: How Single Mothers*

Survive Welfare and Low-Wage Work (Cambridge, MA: Harvard University Press; and New York: Russell Sage Foundation, 1997).

57. Rebecca M. Blank, *It Takes a Nation: A New Agenda for Fighting Poverty* (Princeton, NJ: Princeton University Press, 1997).

58. For an overview and analysis of contemporary changes, see Theda Skocpol, "Advocates Without Members: The Recent Transformation of Civic America," Chapter 13 in *Civic Engagement in American Democracy*, edited by Theda Skocpol and Morris Fiorina (Washington, DC: Brookings Institution Press; and New York: Russell Sage Foundation, 1999).

59. John B. Judis, "The Pressure Elite: Inside the Narrow World of Advocacy Group Politics," *The American Prospect*, number 9 (Spring 1992), pp. 15–29.

60. Jeffrey M. Berry, *Lobbying for the People: The Political Behavior of Public Interest Groups* (Princeton, NJ: Princeton University Press, 1977); and Karen Paget, "Citizen Organizing: Many Movements, No Majority," *The American Prospect*, number 2 (Summer 1990), pp. 115–28.

61. Michael T. Hayes, "The New Group Universe," pp. 133–45 in *Interest Group Politics*, second edition, edited by Allan J. Cigler and Burdett A. Loomis (Washington, DC: CQ Press, 1986).

62. This is massively and meticulously documented in Sidney Verba, Kay Lehman Schlozman, and Henry E. Brady, *Voice and Equality: Civic Voluntarism in American Politics* (Cambridge, MA: Harvard University Press, 1995).

63. Marshall Ganz, "Voters in the Crosshairs: How Technology and the Market Are Destroying Politics," *The American Prospect*, number 16 (Winter 1994), pp. 100–109.

64. Steven J. Rosenstone and John Mark Hansen, *Mobilization, Participation, and Democracy* (New York: Macmillan, 1993).

65. John F. Persinos, "Has the Christian Right Taken Over the Republican Party?," *Campaigns & Elections* 15(9) (September 1994), pp. 20–25.

66. This argument is fully developed in Theda Skocpol, "The GI Bill and U.S. Social Policy, Past and Future," *Social Philosophy & Policy* 14(2) (Summer 1997), pp. 95–115.

67. Alan Brinkley, "Reagan's Revenge: As Invented by Howard Jarvis," *New York Times Magazine*, June 19, 1994.

68. Sidney Blumenthal and Thomas Byrne Edsall, editors, *The Reagan Legacy* (New York: Pantheon Books, 1988).

69. Paul Taylor, "Plight of Children: Seen but Unheeded: Even Madison Avenue Has Trouble Selling Public on Aiding Poor Youth," *Washington Post*, July 15, 1991, p. A4.

70. I develop this argument in *Boomerang: Health Reform and the Turn Against Government* (New York: W. W. Norton, 1997).

CHAPTER THREE

1. Quoted from a 1960 U.S. Senate subcommittee report on "Problems of the Aged and Aging," by Michael Harrington in *The Other America: Poverty in the United States* (New York: Macmillan, 1962), p. 101.
2. Ibid., p. 106.
3. Ibid., p. 105.
4. Ibid., p. 102.
5. Ibid., pp. 104–5.
6. Ibid., pp. 109–14.
7. Ibid., p. 105.
8. Ibid., p. 119.
9. Ibid., p. 118.
10. Ibid., p. 102.
11. Joan Rattner Heilman, *Unbelievably Good Deals . . .* (Chicago, IL: Contemporary Books, 1996). This has been regularly revised since the original 1988 edition.
12. Judith Treas and Ramon Torrecilha, "The Older Population," in *State of the Union: America in the 1990s, Volume Two: Social Trends*, edited by Reynolds Farley (New York: Russell Sage Foundation, 1995), p. 76.
13. Ibid., pp. 72–73, in part quoting from a 1950 census monograph on the older population, Henry D. Sheldon, *The Older Population in the United States* (New York: Wiley, 1958), pp. 40–41.
14. Ibid., p. 73.
15. Paul Taylor, "The Coming Conflict as We Soak the Young to Enrich the Old," *Washington Post*, January 5, 1986, p. D1. The article itself is more nuanced than the headline suggests.
16. Neil Howe and Phillip Longman, "The Next New Deal," *The Atlantic*, 269(4) (April 1992), pp. 90, 96.
17. Lester C. Thurow, "The Birth of a Revolutionary Class," *New York Times Magazine*, May 19, 1996, pp. 46–47.
18. *Newsweek*, September 18, 1995.
19. Paul Magnusson, "Victims of the Golden Years," *Business Week*, May 22, 1995, p. 44.
20. Margot Hornblower, "Gray Power! AARP Emerges as the Nation's Most Powerful Special-Interest Lobby," *Time*, January 4, 1988, pp. 36–37.
21. Lee Smith, "The World According to AARP," *Fortune*, February 29, 1988, p. 96. This image may say more about the extended families of people who read *Fortune* magazine than it does about the influence of grandfathers in average American families!
22. Treas and Torrecilha, "Older Population," pp. 62–63.
23. U.S. Senate Special Committee on Aging, American Association of Retired Persons, Federal Council on Aging, and the U.S. Administration on Aging, *Aging America: Trends and Projections*, 1991 edition

(Washington, DC: U.S. Department of Health and Human Services, 1991), pp. 112–15. See also Urie Bronfenbrenner, Peter McLelland, Elaine Wethington, Phyllis Moen, and Stephen J. Ceci, *The State of Americans: This Generation and the Next* (New York: The Free Press, 1996), Figure 7-9, p. 219.

24. Ibid., pp. 111–12.
25. Ibid., pp. 108–10.
26. Trip Gabriel, "Holiday Travelers Make Room for Grandma," *New York Times*, July 14, 1996, pp. 1, 20.
27. Treas and Torrecilha, "Older Population," pp. 73–74.
28. Ibid., p. 77.
29. Ibid., p. 69.
30. Dowell Myers and Jennifer R. Wolch, "The Polarization of Housing Status," in *State of the Union: America in the 1990s, Volume One: Economic Trends*, edited by Reynolds Farley (New York: Russell Sage Foundation, 1995), pp. 279, 294–96.
31. Edward N. Wolff, *Top Heavy: A Study of the Increasing Inequality of Wealth in America*, A Twentieth Century Fund Report (New York: Twentieth Century Fund Press, 1995), pp. 16–17, 19, including Figure 4-1.
32. *Aging America*, 1991 edition, p. 76.
33. Treas and Torrecilha, "Older Population," pp. 84–85, including Figure 2.12. See also the interesting data presented in Timothy M. Smeeding, "Economic Status of the Elderly," in *Handbook of Aging and the Social Sciences*, third edition, edited by Robert H. Binstock and Linda K. George (New York: Academic Press, 1990), pp. 366–67.
34. Sheldon Danziger and Peter Gottschalk, *America Unequal* (Cambridge, MA: Harvard University Press; and New York: Russell Sage Foundation, 1995), p. 72.
35. Treas and Torrecilha, "Older Population," p. 78.
36. *Aging America*, 1991 edition, Table 2-2, p. 41.
37. Ibid., pp. xxi, 80–81.
38. Treas and Torrecilha, "Older Population," p. 81; *Aging America*, 1991 edition, Chart 2-11, p. 55.
39. See such news articles and analyses as: "Heat Now Being Counted in Bodies, Not Degrees," *Chicago Tribune*, July 17, 1995; "The Heat Wave's Victims," *Chicago Tribune*, November 26, 1995; and "Dissecting a Heat Wave," *New York Times*, October 4, 1995, p. A2.
40. "8-Day Heat Wave Claims 20 Victims in Texas and Oklahoma," *New York Times*, July 14, 1996, section 1, p. 24.
41. Treas and Torrecilha, "Older Population," Figure 2.10, p. 80.
42. Lisa Genasci, "Women Less-Prepared for Retirement," *Boston Globe*, July 23, 1995, p. 73.

43. See findings from the research of Linda Waite, as discussed in Jennifer Steinhauer, "Studies Find Big Benefits in Marriage," *New York Times*, April 10, 1995, p. A10, and in Lee A. Lillard and Linda J. Waite, "'Til Death Do Us Part: Marital Disruption and Mortality," *American Journal of Sociology 100*(5) (March 1995), pp. 1131–56.

44. Robert L. Clark, "Income Maintenance Policies in the United States," in *Handbook of Aging and the Social Sciences*, edited by Binstock and George, p. 384.

45. Danziger and Gottschalk, *America Unequal*, p. 84.

46. Ibid.

47. Clark, "Income Maintenance Policies," p. 389.

48. Ibid., p. 390; and Lawrence Mishel, Jared Bernstein, and John Schmitt, *The State of Working America, 1998–99* (Ithaca, NY: Cornell University Press, 1999), pp. 143–48.

49. Clark, "Income Maintenance Policies," pp. 393–95.

50. Stanley B. Greenberg, "The Economy Project" (Washington, DC: Greenberg Research, January 16, 1996), p. 58.

51. Danziger and Gottschalk, *America Unequal*, p. 83.

52. Ibid.

53. Ibid.

54. Ibid., p. 84.

55. Ibid., pp. 83–84.

56. *Medicare Reform: A Twentieth Century Fund Guide to the Basic Issues* (New York: Twentieth Century Fund Press, 1995), p. 6.

57. Ibid., p. 26.

58. See Marilyn Moon, *Medicare Now and in the Future* (Washington, DC: The Urban Institute Press, 1993), pp. 10–12; and the discussion of the Families USA study by Charlotte Grimes, "Elderly Spent More in '91 on Health than in 1961, Study Finds," *St. Louis Post-Dispatch*, February 26, 1992, Five Star Edition, p. 1C.

59. *Aging America*, 1991 edition, pp. 138–39.

60. *Medicaid Reform: A Twentieth Century Fund Guide to the Basic Issues* (New York: Twentieth Century Fund Press, 1995), p. 10.

61. Treas and Torrecilha, "Older Population," p. 63.

62. *Medicare Reform*, p. 11.

63. Peter G. Peterson, *Facing Up: How to Rescue the Economy from Crushing Debt and Restore the American Dream* (New York: Simon and Schuster, 1993), p. 82. Notice the exaggeration in the statement that elder advocacy organizations claim a "combined membership of 100 million." Obviously, many older Americans belong to several of these groups.

64. Paul E. Peterson, "An Immodest Proposal," *The Brookings Review 11*(1) (Winter 1993), p. 23. Another version of the same article appeared in an issue of *Daedalus* on "Immobile Democracy?," *121*(4) (Fall 1992),

pp. 151–74. In the fine print, it turns out that Peterson really wants to give parents considerable discretion over their children's voting rights.

65. Charles R. Morris, *The AARP: America's Most Powerful Lobby and the Clash of Generations* (New York: Times Books, 1996), Chapter 1.

66. These quotes and figures come from Chapter 2 of a draft Ph.D. dissertation, Andrea L. Campbell's "Linking Participation and Policy: Senior Citizen Activism and the American Welfare State" (Department of Political Science, University of California at Berkeley, 1999). Campbell uses self-reported voting participation rates from the National Election Study.

67. Fay Lomax Cook and Edith J. Barrett, *Support for the American Welfare State: The Views of Congress and the Public* (New York: Columbia University Press, 1992), p. 164.

68. Quoted in ibid.

69. Robert Blendon, "What Happened to Americans' Support of the Clinton Plan?," *Health Affairs* 14(2) (Summer 1995), especially Exhibit 1, p. 10.

70. Norman Ornstein, "Flashback," *The New Republic*, July 3, 1995, pp. 16–19; and Ruy Teixeira, "Who Rejoined the Democrats? Understanding the 1996 Election Results," Briefing Paper (Washington, DC: The Economic Policy Institute, November 1996).

71. This paragraph draws especially upon Christine L. Day, *What Older Americans Think: Interest Groups and Aging Policy* (Princeton, NJ: Princeton University Press, 1990), Chapter 3 on "Political Attitudes of the Elderly."

72. This argument is made and documented in Andrea L. Campbell, "Linking Participation and Policy."

73. Ibid.; and Cook and Barrett, *Support for the American Welfare State*, Table 5.2, p. 154.

74. Leora Lawton, Merril Silverstein, and Vern L. Bengston, "Solidarity Between Generations in Families," pp. 19–42 in *Intergenerational Linkages: Hidden Connections in American Society*, edited by Vern L. Bengston and Robert A. Harootyan (New York: Springer Publishing Company, 1994).

75. Lawton, Silverstein, and Bengston, "Solidarity," p. 26.

76. Ibid., p. 42.

77. *Aging America*, 1991 edition, pp. 202–5; Thomas M. Guterbock and John C. Fries, "Maintaining America's Social Fabric: The AARP Survey of Civic Involvement" (Washington, DC: American Association of Retired Persons, 1997); and Marc Freedman, "The Aging Opportunity: America's Elderly as a Civic Resource," *The American Prospect*, number 29 (November–December 1996), pp. 44–52.

78. Karl Kronebusch and Mark Schlesinger, "Intergenerational Transfers,"

in *Intergenerational Linkages*, edited by Bengston and Harootyan, pp. 148–49.

79. Henry J. Pratt, *Gray Agendas: Interest Groups and Public Pensions in Canada, Britain, and the United States* (Ann Arbor: University of Michigan Press, 1993), pp. 179–80.

80. Henry J. Pratt, *The Gray Lobby* (Chicago, IL: University of Chicago Press, 1976), pp. 88–89.

81. Ibid., pp. 154–68.

82. Martha Derthick, *Policymaking for Social Security* (Washington, DC: Brookings Institution Press, 1979).

83. Theodore R. Marmor, *The Politics of Medicare* (Chicago, IL: Aldine, 1970).

84. Lawrence R. Jacobs, *The Health of Nations: Public Opinion and the Making of American and British Health Policy* (Ithaca, NY: Cornell University Press, 1993), Chapters 3, 5, 7, and 9.

85. Pratt, *Gray Lobby*, Chapter 5 and pp. 88–89.

86. On the AARP's origins, see Morris, *The AARP*, Chapter 2; Margaret Abrams, *The Story of AARP* (Washington, DC: American Association of Retired Persons, 1971); and Pratt, *Gray Lobby*, Chapter 7.

87. Pratt, *Gray Lobby*, p. 91.

88. Henry J. Pratt, "National Interest Groups Among the Elderly: Consolidation and Constraint," in *Aging and Public Policy: The Politics of Growing Old in America*, edited by William P. Browne and Laura Katz Olson (Westport, CT: Greenwood Press, 1983), p. 157.

89. Neal R. Peirce and Peter C. Choharis, "The Elderly as a Political Force . . .," *The National Journal*, September 11, 1982, pp. 1559–62.

90. Debra Street, "Maintaining the Status Quo: The Impact of Old-Age Interest Groups on the Medicare Catastrophic Coverage Act of 1988," *Social Problems* 40(4) (November 1993), pp. 431–44.

91. Robert Pear, "Clinton Fails to Get Endorsement of Elderly Group on Health Plan," *New York Times*, February 25, 1994, pp. A1, A15.

92. I tell the full story in my book, *Boomerang: Health Reform and the Turn Against Government* (New York: W. W. Norton, 1997). My main discussion of the AARP appears on pages 92–95.

93. Hoary projections of this sort are staples for Peter Peterson of the Concord Coalition, for many conservative Republicans and new Democrats, and for Ross Perot (who illustrated his mid-1990s budget talks with charts borrowed from Peter Peterson).

94. Very helpful discussions of where different demographic, economic, and fiscal projections come from—and how widely they can vary—appear in Robert B. Friedland and Laura Summer, *Demography Is Not Destiny* (Washington, DC: National Academy on an Aging Society, 1999).

95. *Aging America*, 1991 edition, p. 19; and Richard C. Leone, "Why the Boomers Don't Spell Bust," *American Prospect* 30 (January–February 1997), pp. 68–71.

96. *Social Security: A Guide to the Issues* (New York: Twentieth Century Fund Press, 1996), Figure 1, p. 17.

97. See "Economic Growth Matters," Chapter 3 in Friedland and Summer, *Demography Is Not Destiny*.

98. Kingson and Quadagno, "Marketing Radical Reform"; and Thomas Conley Rollins, Jr. "The New Politics of Social Security" (Unpublished Senior Honors Essay, Harvard College, March 1998).

99. Robert Pear, "Panel Nears Consensus on Redesigning Medicare," *New York Times*, January 27, 1999. The headline is misleading about the degree of unity on this commission, as Pear's text makes clear. See also Amy Goldstein, "Medicare Reform Panel Split: Discord Centers on Which Benefits to Guarantee," *Washington Post*, January 27, 1999, p. A2.

100. Kip Sullivan, "Bad Prescription: Why Privatizing Medicare May Be Hazardous to Your Health," *Washington Monthly 31*(3) (March 1999), p. 27. This article includes an excellent discussion of how Medicare has done a better job than private insurance of controlling costs without excluding patients.

101. *Report of the 1994–1996 Advisory Council on Social Security, Volume 1: Findings and Recommendations* (Washington, DC: Social Security Administration, January 1997). For useful discussions and comparisons of the alternate reform plans put forward by Advisory Council members, see Joseph F. Quinn and Olivia S. Mitchell, "Social Security on the Table," *The American Prospect*, number 26 (May–June 1996); pp. 76–81; and *Social Security Reform: A Twentieth Century Fund Guide to the Issues* (New York: Twentieth Century Fund Press, 1996).

102. On total individualization as envisaged by Milton Friedman, see his "Social Security Chimeras," *New York Times*, January 11, 1999, p. A21. On proposals presented by Martin Feldstein at a White House conference on Social Security reform, see Michael M. Weinstein, "Poof! You Can Retire Rich," *New York Times*, December 20, 1998, Week in Review, p. 6; and Robert Greenstein, Wendell Primus, and Kilolo Kijakazi, "The Feldstein Social Security Plan" (Washington, DC: Center on Budget and Policy Priorities, December 16, 1998).

103. Robert J. Shapiro, "A New Deal on Social Security," pp. 39–55 in *Building the Bridge: Ten Big Ideas to Transform America*, edited by Will Marshall (Lanham, MD: Rowman and Littlefield, 1997).

104. On the crucial yet quiet role that Wall Street interests have played in encouraging privatization, see Robert Dreyfuss, "The Real Threat to Social Security," *The Nation*, February 8, 1999, p. 15

CHAPTER FOUR

1. *Beyond Rhetoric: A New American Agenda for Children and Families*, Final Report of the National Commission on Children (Washington, DC: U.S. Government Printing Office, 1991), p. 7. Chaired by West Virginia Senator John D. Rockefeller IV, the thirty-two member Commission included the well-known author of child-rearing manuals, pediatrician T. Berry Brazelton; the liberal icon of child advocates, Marian Wright Edelman; a major conservative advocate for families, Allan Carlson of the Rockford Institute; business leader Irving B. Harris of the Pittway Corporation; the then-Governor of Arkansas Bill Clinton; and many other leaders from the worlds of social service, charity, business, and politics.

   For a discussion of the Commission's recommendations and what has become of them, see Irwin Garfinkel, "Economic Security for Children: From Means Testing to Universality," in *Social Policies for Children*, edited by Irwin Garfinkel, Jennifer L. Hochschild, and Sara S. McLanahan (Washington, DC: Brookings Institution Press, 1996).

2. Examples (from among many possible) include: *Starting Points: Meeting the Needs of Our Youngest Children*, Report of the Carnegie Task Force on Meeting the Needs of Young Children (New York: Carnegie Corporation of New York, 1994); the "Kids Count" reports of the Annie Casey Foundation; and "The Future of Children" publications of the David and Lucile Packard Foundation. The American Academy of Arts and Sciences sponsors "Initiatives for Children" reports and projects. Even groups originally focused on programs for the elderly have taken up the children's theme. For example, the National Academy of Social Insurance, built around Social Security, focused an annual meeting on children; see Paul N. Van de Water and Lisbeth B. Schorr, *Security for America's Children: Proceedings of the Fourth Conference of the National Academy of Social Insurance* (Dubuque, IA: Kendall/Hunt Publishing Company, 1992).

3. For some examples, see Sylvia Ann Hewlett, *When the Bough Breaks: The Costs of Neglecting Our Children* (New York: Basic Books, 1991); Richard Louv, *Childhood's Future* (New York: Doubleday, 1991); Penelope Leach, *Children First: What Our Society Must Do—and Is Not Doing—For Our Children Today* (New York: Knopf, 1994); and James Garbarino, *Raising Children in a Socially Toxic Environment* (San Francisco, CA: Jossey-Bass, 1995).

4. For the Democrats, see Democratic Congressional Campaign, "Families First Agenda: Fighting for America's Working Families" (Washington, DC: Office of the Democratic Leader, U.S. House of Representatives, 1996). On the conservative side see, for example, Representative Henry Hyde, "A Mom and Pop Manifesto: What the Pro-Family Move-

ment Wants from Congress," *Policy Review* 68 (Spring 1994), pp. 29–33.

5. Garfinkel, "Security for Children," discusses the "U-shaped" structure of many U.S. benefit and income-support policies, showing that benefits flow disproportionately to the top and bottom fifths of the population.

6. This point is persuasively made by Ben J. Wattenberg, *Values Matter Most* (New York: Free Press, 1995), Chapter 4, specifically pp. 86–87. However, as will become apparent, I do not agree with Wattenberg's overall argument that economic trends are irrelevant to families' worries and well-being.

7. Lee Rainwater and Timothy M. Smeeding, "Doing Poorly: The Real Income of American Children in a Comparative Perspective," Working Paper No. 127 (Syracuse, NY: Maxwell School of Citizenship and Public Affairs, Syracuse University, August 1995).

8. Ibid., p. 9.

9. For a summary of poverty trends by age groups from 1959 to 1996, see Figure 4.3 in Robert B. Friedland and Laura Summer, *Demography Is Not Destiny* (Washington, DC: National Academy on an Aging Society, 1999), p. 32. Note that official U.S. poverty statistics are not exactly the same as those used in the Luxembourg Income Study. The latter includes more in-kind and tax-credit sources of income.

10. Garbarino, *Raising Children in a Socially Toxic Environment*, p. 136.

11. Ibid., citing M. Bane and D. Ellwood, "Slipping Into and Out of Poverty: The Dynamics of Spells" (Cambridge, MA: National Bureau of Economic Research, 1989).

12. Urie Bronfenbrenner, Peter McLelland, Elaine Wethington, Phyllis Moen, and Stephen J. Ceci, *The State of Americans: This Generation and the Next* (New York: Free Press, 1996), p. 158, Figure 5-7.

13. In addition to the citations below, see the issue on "Children and Poverty" of *The Future of Children* 7(2) (Summer/Fall 1997).

14. Bronfenbrenner et al., *State of Americans*, p. 52. See also Sheldon Danziger and Peter Gottschalk, *America Unequal* (Cambridge, MA: Harvard University Press; and New York: Russell Sage Foundation, 1995). In cross-national perspective, rising income inequality in the United States is especially glaring. See Anthony Atkinson, Lee Rainwater, and Timothy Smeeding, "Income Distribution in Advanced Economies: Evidence from the Luxembourg Income Study," Working Paper No. 120 (Syracuse, NY: Maxwell School of Citizenship and Public Affairs, Syracuse University, October 1995).

15. Judith Waldrop, "It's a Struggle," *American Demographics* 12(2) (February 1990); Susan D. Einbinder and James T. Bond, "Young Children Still Live in Poverty—Despite Parental Employment," *Child Poverty*

News & Issues 3(1) (Winter/Spring 1993); "Report: Incomes Fall for Parents Under 30," *Newsday*, September 17, 1997, p. A46; Edward N. Wolff, "Economic Status of Parents in Postwar America," Discussion Paper (New York: National Parenting Association, September 1996); and David T. Ellwood, "Winners and Losers in America: Taking the Measure of the New Economic Realities," forthcoming in a book to be published by the Russell Sage Foundation, New York City.

16. Kathryn Edin and Laura Lein, *Making Ends Meet: How Single Mothers Survive Welfare and Low-Wage Work* (Cambridge, MA: Harvard University Press; and New York: Russell Sage Foundation, 1997).

17. Danziger and Gottschalk, *America Unequal*, pp. 83–85.

18. Rainwater and Smeeding, "Doing Poorly," p. 20.

19. Bronfenbrenner et al., *State of Americans*, Figure 3-7, p. 65; Figure 5-11, p. 164.

20. Sheila B. Kammerman, "Women, Children, and Poverty: Public Policies and Female-headed Families in Industrialized Countries," pp. 41–63 in *Women and Poverty*, edited by Barbara C. Gelpi, Nancy C. M. Hartsock, Clare C. Novak, and Myra H. Strober (Chicago, IL: University of Chicago Press, 1986). See also Michael O'Higgins, "The Allocation of Public Resources to Children and the Elderly in OECD Countries," pp. 201–28; and Sheila B. Kammerman and Alfred J. Kahn, "Social Policy and Children in the United States and Europe," pp. 351–80, both in *The Vulnerable*, edited by John L. Palmer, Timothy Smeeding, and Barbara Boyle Torrey (Washington, DC: The Urban Institute Press, 1988).

21. Jack A. Meyer and Marilyn Moon, "Health Care Spending on Children and the Elderly," pp. 171–200 in *The Vulnerable*, edited by Palmer, Smeeding, and Torrey; and Barbara R. Bergmann, *Saving Our Children from Poverty: What the United States Can Learn from France* (New York: Russell Sage Foundation, 1996).

22. Ruth Sidel, *Keeping Women and Children Last: America's War on the Poor* (New York: Penguin Books, 1996), pp. xx–xxi.

23. See Garfinkel, "Security for Children," on these patterns, which divide the very poor from the near-poor and the lower middle class.

24. Paul Taylor, "Plight of Children Seen but Unheeded: Even Madison Avenue Has Trouble Selling Public on Aiding Poor Youth," *Washington Post*, July 15, 1991, p. A4.

25. For a discussion of the complex crosscurrents in American opinions about children and the adults attached to them, see H. Hugh Heclo, "Values Underpinning Poverty Programs for Children," *The Future of Children* (Children and Poverty) 7(2) (Summer/Fall 1997), pp. 141–48.

26. George Gilder, "The Roots of Black Poverty," *Wall Street Journal*, October 30, 1995, p. A18.

27. Charles Murray, "The Coming White Underclass," *Wall Street Journal*, October 29, 1993, p. A14, and "And Now for the Bad News," *Wall Street Journal*, February 2, 1999, p. A22.

28. Wattenberg, *Values Matter Most*, p. 93.

29. David Popenoe, *Life Without Father: Compelling New Evidence that Fatherhood and Marriage Are Indispensable for the Good of Children and Society* (New York: Free Press, 1996), p. 1.

30. Ibid., p. 13.

31. Ibid., p. 3.

32. Ibid., pp. 22–23.

33. Ibid., p. 23

34. Bronfenbrenner et al., *State of Americans*, p. 92, Figure 4-1.

35. Ibid., p. 93, Figure 4-1; and Sara McLanahan and Lynn Casper, "Growing Diversity and Inequality in the American Family," Table 1.2, p. 15, in *State of the Union: America in the 1990s, Volume Two: Social Trends*, edited by Reynolds Farley (New York: Russell Sage Foundation, 1995).

36. Bronfenbrenner et al., *State of Americans*, Figure 4-6, p. 98.

37. McLanahan and Casper, "Growing Diversity," p. 15.

38. Popenoe, *Life Without Father*, pp. 22–23, citing Sandra L. Hofferth, "Updating Children's Life Course," *Journal of Marriage and the Family* 47 (1985), pp. 93–115. See also *Kids Count: A Pocket Guide to America's Youth* (Baltimore, MD: Annie E. Casey Foundation, 1995).

39. Popenoe, *Life Without Father*, p. 33.

40. Ibid.

41. Sara McLanahan and Gary Sandefur, *Growing Up with a Single Parent: What Hurts, What Helps* (Cambridge, MA: Harvard University Press, 1994).

42. Ibid., pp. 23–26. This paragraph and the next also draw upon Mary Jo Bane, "Marital Disruption and the Lives of Children," *Journal of Social Issues* 32(1) (1976), pp. 103–17.

43. "Children and Divorce," issue of *The Future of Children* 4(1) (Spring 1994), p. 6. For the full analysis, see an article in the issue, Jay D. Teachman and Kathleen Paasch, "Financial Impact of Divorce on Children and Their Families."

44. Edin and Lein, *Making Ends Meet*, Chapter 4.

45. For a full analysis, see Paula G. Roberts, "Child Support Orders: Problems with Enforcement," *The Future of Children* 4(1) (Spring 1994), pp. 101–20.

46. Bronfenbrenner et al., *State of Americans*, Figure 5-13, p. 166.

47. Popenoe, *Life Without Father*, p. 31.

48. Ibid., p. 44; and Bronfenbrenner et al., *State of Americans*, Figure 5-11, p. 164.

49. Popenoe, *Life Without Father*, p. 35. For a fuller discussion of unmarried motherhood, see Kristin Luker, *Dubious Conceptions: The Politics of Teenage Pregnancy* (Cambridge, MA: Harvard University Press, 1996).

50. Popenoe, *Life Without Father*, p. 44.

51. Ibid., p. 45, citing Daniel Yankelovich, "How Changes in the Economy Are Reshaping American Values," pp. 16–53 in *Values and Public Policy*, edited by Henry J. Aaron, Thomas Mann, and Timothy Taylor (Washington, DC: The Brookings Institution, 1994).

52. Popenoe, *Life Without Father*, p. 47.

53. Ibid., p. 45.

54. See ibid., pp. 220–23; and William A. Galston, "Needed: A Not-So-Fast Divorce Law," *New York Times*, December 27, 1995, p. A15. See also Dirk Johnson, "No-Fault Divorce Is Under Attack," *New York Times*, February 12, 1996, p. A10.

55. Sylvia Ann Hewlett and Cornel West, *The War Against Parents: What We Can Do for America's Beleaguered Moms and Dads* (Boston, MA: Houghton Mifflin, 1998), Chapter 7.

56. Danziger and Gottschalk, *America Unequal*, p. 106. The authors claim that their decomposition shows "family structure changes were important, but they were less important than economic changes." I doubt we can make such fine-grained estimations. Their analysis, to my mind, shows that both effects were massive. And it cannot explore the subtle ways that economic and social and cultural transformations were intertwined over time.

57. Bronfenbrenner et al., *State of Americans*, Chapter 5.

58. The most recent analysis underlining this conclusion is Ellwood, "Winners and Losers."

59. Garbarino, *Raising Children in a Socially Toxic Environment*, p. 141.

60. Donald J. Hernandez, *America's Children: Resources from Family, Government, and the Economy* (New York: Russell Sage Foundation, 1993), p. 99. For an excellent overview, see all of Chapter 4 on "Parents' Work and the Family Economy Twice Transformed."

61. McLanahan and Casper, "Growing Diversity," pp. 12–13.

62. Ellwood, "Winners and Losers."

63. Ibid.

64. Danziger and Gottschalk, *America Unequal*, p. 114. See also Ellwood, "Winners and Losers."

65. Bronfenbrenner et al., *State of Americans*, Figure 4-12, p. 108.

66. Richard Morin, "How the Haves and Have-Nots Differ: A Survey Shows the Poor—Particularly Adults—Are Under Great Strain," *Washington Post National Weekly Edition*, February 1, 1999, p. 35.

67. Orlando Patterson, "The Crisis of Gender Relations Among African

Americans" (unpublished typescript, Department of Sociology, Harvard University).

68. Dirk Johnson, "Family Struggles to Make Do After Fall from Middle Class," *New York Times*, March 11, 1994, pp. A1, A14.

69. Ibid., p. A14.

70. Ibid.

71. Ibid.

72. This thesis is eloquently argued in another book written as I was doing this one: Hewlett and West, *War Against Parents*.

73. U.S. Bureau of the Census, data on Internet, released July 3, 1997.

74. Victor R. Fuchs, "Are Americans Underinvesting in Their Children?," *Society* 28(6) (September/October 1991), p. 22.

75. Paul Adams, "Children as Contributions in Kind: Social Security and Family Policy," *Social Work* 35(6) (November 1990), pp. 492–97.

76. Hernandez, *America's Children*, Chapter 2.

77. Dennis P. Hogan and Daniel T. Lichter, "Children and Youth: Living Arrangements and Welfare," in *State of the Union, Volume Two: Social Trends*, edited by Farley, p. 100.

78. Fuchs, "Americans Underinvesting?," p. 20.

79. Mark Lind, "Expenditures on Children by Families," 1997 Annual Report, U.S. Department of Agriculture, Center for Nutrition Policy and Promotion, Miscellaneous Publication No. 1528-1997 (Washington, DC: USDA, 1998).

80. Fuchs, "Americans Underinvesting?," p. 20.

81. Hewlett and West, *War Against Parents*, p. 259.

82. Juliet B. Schor, *The Overworked American: The Unexpected Decline of Leisure* (New York: Basic Books, 1991), Chapter 2. The following paragraphs also draw upon Juliet B. Schor, "Short of Time: American Families and the Structure of Jobs" (Harvard University, Committee on Women's Studies, March 1994 typescript); and Schor, "Time Crunch Among American Parents" (New York: National Parenting Association, 1998).

83. Cited in Schor, "Short of Time."

84. Hewlett and West, *War Against Parents*, p. 259.

85. For a full discussion, see Juliet B. Schor, *The Overspent American: Upscaling, Downshifting, and the New Consumer* (New York: Basic Books, 1998).

86. I draw upon Allan Carlson, "Taxes and the Family" (New York: National Parenting Association, 1996).

87. David E. Rosenbaum, "Social Security: The Basics, With a Tally Sheet," *New York Times*, January 28, 1999, p. A19. As this article spells out, 62 percent of Social Security recipients in December 1998 were retired

workers; 7 percent were the spouses and children of retired workers; 16 percent were the spouses and children of deceased workers; 11 percent were disabled people; and 4 percent were spouses and children of disabled people.

CHAPTER FIVE

1. I have changed the names of my son's friend and his mother.
2. Robert Pear, "Government Lags in Steps to Widen Health Coverage," *New York Times*, August 9, 1998, pp. 1, 22. See also my discussion and notes in Chapter 1.
3. See the views reported in Sylvia Ann Hewlett and Cornel West, *The War Against Parents: What We Can Do for America's Beleaguered Moms and Dads* (Boston, MA: Houghton Mifflin, 1998), Appendix A; and in the W. K. Kellogg Foundation's "Devolution Survey on Healthcare and Welfare Reform Issues," released January 13, 1999.
4. This is carefully explained in Kip Sullivan, "Bad Prescription: Why Privatizing Medicare May Be Hazardous to Your Health," *Washington Monthly 31*(3) (March 1999), pp. 27–32.
5. *Social Security Reform: A Twentieth Century Fund Guide to the Issues* (New York: Twentieth Century Fund Press, 1996), p. 6.
6. The original version of this plan is spelled out in Barry Bluestone, Alan Clayton-Matthews, John Havens, and Howard Young, "Generational Alliance: Social Security as a Bank for Education and Training," *The American Prospect*, number 2 (Summer 1990), pp. 15–29.
7. Irwin Garfinkel, *Assuring Child Support: An Extension of Social Security* (New York: Russell Sage Foundation, 1992).
8. Center on Budget and Policy Priorities, "Assessing a $5.15-an-hour Minimum Wage," Washington, DC, March 27, 1996.
9. Barbara R. Bergmann, "Child Care: The Key to Ending Child Poverty," pp. 112–35 in *Social Policies for Children*, edited by Irwin Garfinkel, Jennifer L. Hochschild, and Sara S. McLanahan (Washington, DC: Brookings Institution Press, 1996).
10. Richard B. Freeman, editor, *Working Under Different Rules* (New York: Russell Sage Foundation, 1994).
11. Following the lead of most elected Democrats in recent years, progressives can also support tough crime laws and active measures to make neighborhoods safe, clean, and orderly. And we can agree to hold public schools to high standards, even as we seek funds to pay for small classes and creative teachers. I do not dwell on such matters in this book about national-level social policy, because they are matters largely addressed by localities and states. But national politics has a supportive role to play, just as governments at all levels must have the wherewithal and inspiration to encourage private sector and voluntary

activities to nurture and supervise children—and to honor and support mother and fathers.

12. On this point, see William Julius Wilson, *The Bridge Over the Racial Divide: Rising Inequality and Coalition Politics* (Berkeley and Los Angeles: University of California Press, forthcoming Fall 1999).

13. *Tenth Anniversary Edition of Economic Justice for All: Pastoral Letter on Catholic Social Teaching and the U.S. Economy* (Washington, DC: United States Catholic Conference, 1997), p. 1.

14. Margaret Weir and Marshall Ganz, "Reconnecting People and Politics," pp. 149–71 in *The New Majority: Toward a Popular Progressive Politics*, edited by Stanley B. Greenberg and Theda Skocpol (New Haven, CT: Yale University Press, 1997).

15. For a full discussion, see Theda Skocpol, "How Americans Became Civic," in *Civic Engagement in American Democracy*, edited by Theda Skocpol and Morris Fiorina (Washington, DC: Brookings Institution Press; and New York: Russell Sage Foundation, 1999). Changes in U.S. civic life since the 1960s are discussed in Theda Skocpol, "Advocates without Members," another chapter in the same book.

16. Hewlett and West, *War Against Parents*, Part IV.

INDEX